The book is not a DIY manual on house renovation, however, it does contain information that would be useful for those starting out on similar projects.

It is a light-hearted story of when my husband and I spent two years working on an old farmhouse in the southern part of Brittany.
We changed a two hundred year old building, with some dirt floors, holes in the roof, woodworm in the beams and rotten floorboards into a home with a comfortable interior whilst retaining the original character of the building.

It tells of satisfaction, disappointment, fun, enjoyment, frustration, difficulties, doubts and hopes along the way. We experienced the generosity of the local French people and their willingness to give help when needed. It was rural life at its best within a farming community, realising this when a cow delivered her calf in front of our doorstep.

The house is in the hamlet of Quelneuc, by the Lac au Duc, which is a large lake and within 40 minutes drive from west coast of France.

Names of individual characters featured in the book have not been changed as I wish to acknowledge their part in the story.

The question was it all worth while is for readers to make informed decisions based on their own circumstances.

The French Renovation

How We Renovated a House in France

by

Jill McNicoll

Publisher: Whitehouse Books
Telephone 01905 821110

The French Renovation

Published by

*Whitehouse Books
Clareland
Old Road South
Kempsey
Worcestershire
WR5 3NJ
Telephone 01905 821110*

Copyright © Jill McNicoll 2003

Illustrations Copyright © Jill Whitehouse 2000

ISBN: 0-9544593-0-X

Printed in England by: ProntaPrint----Worcester

Chapters

1 Early Connections with France

2 Buying the House

3 Renovating without a Toilet

4 Topless near St Nazaire

5 The Straw Man

6 Water Down the Chimney

7 The Dawn Patrol

8 Stuck in the Mud

9 Water in the Diesel

10 Peaches with Everything

11 Quelneuc not Carnac

12 Plastered at Last

13 Twinkle Toes & Tequila

14 Suzannah & Emma

15 Call a Halt and Sell

16 The Mouse Returns

17 Was It Worth It?

Chapter One

Early connections with France

At times during my life I have had connections with France. They began as a four-year-old child when I commenced my education at a boarding school in a convent run by a French order of nuns of the Holy Trinity in Worcestershire. My father wished me to have an all round education which included spiritual guidance. I can remember how the nuns spoke to each other in these strange words that later I was to learn was the French language. Our prayers were recited in French which I remember to this day. It is a pity that the pupils did not learn more of the French language at an early age.

When I was 12 years of age my parents moved to the Isle of Wight where I became a day scholar at the Presentation Convent. Here I met Mother Finbar who was one of the nuns who taught me. This lady was a big influence in my life, supporting me when I needed help. She was the person who arranged for me to visit France on a school trip to Lourdes. I remember her face so clearly. Her skin looked just like alabaster and reminded me of the Virgin Mary statue, which I still have on a shelf over the ancient inglenook in our house in France. In later years I learned that she had been dying of leukaemia. Perhaps I could say that it was Mother Finbar who first aroused my interest in France.

Many years later, during summer holidays, I stayed with an uncle who had retired to France and lived in a delightful little bungalow on the banks of the river Cher, just outside the town of Vierzon in the Loire Valley. He had finally settled in this area after travelling to many parts of the world because his sister lived there and their French mother had lived there before she had married a Scot. My uncle had spent his early years in Scotland. When I went on holiday to France, my uncle would take me on day excursions to places of local interest such as Orleans and Bourges. He spoke fluent French that enabled me to discover more about France and its people. In the evenings we would take our cold drinks and sit out on the small balcony overlooking the river. I remember as it became dusk we would watch the river creatures playing on the lily pads on the opposite side of the Cher. The river was wide and fast running so if the odd water rat appeared it was far enough away for me not to feel threatened. Sadly my uncle died in very strange circumstances.

He had been to the bank to get his pension and as far as we know, he returned home, disappeared and his little West Highland terrier dog was seen wandering along the riverbank. Two weeks later his body was found in the river and the police suspected foul play. His house had signs of a break-in and there was none of his money found. He had been seen wearing his sheepskin coat on the day that he had gone missing, but the coat was not found and the mystery was never solved. I remember returning to his house just after his funeral. The house, which had been so cheerful and full of laughter, was now silent and the feeling of intense loneliness swept over me. I walked outside glad to be in the sunlight, pausing by the river and looking down into the deep water I shivered as memories of my uncle came flooding back. He had been so full of life and always such a generous person - how could this dreadful thing have happened to him. I recalled the day we had spent shopping with him the day when he had bought the expensive sheepskin coat. It was strange that this should be the article of clothing to go missing. They say time is a great healer and memories become less painful, but on that day I felt I would never return to France.

Many years later, Fran and Derek, who had been friends of ours for years, bought a French property in the region of Deux Sevres. This house was virtually unchanged since the eighteenth century and therefore was a major renovation project. We had stayed at their house for holidays always loving their way of life in France. It was so relaxing compared with our life in England - somehow it always seemed warmer and the pace of living was slower. We loved the vin rouge and the paté and of course the crêpes were a delight.

Over the time of our visits, we were interested in watching their house improve and become a desirable property. Obviously this had taken hard work and expenditure but everyone said that the result was worth the effort.

My husband and I had discussed the possibility of doing the same as our friends and buying a house when we retired. Like Fran I had worked most of my life in the National Health Service and I would receive a lump sum on retirement and what better way to spend it - Vive la France. We were not afraid to take on this type of project since my husband had much previous house building and renovation experience in the UK. This type of project in France would require different methods, planning and skills especially if we were starting from thick stone walls and dirt floors.

In the summer of 1996 my husband and I, son Richard, his partner Michelle and three grandchildren, went for a holiday to France. We rented a gîte at St Yvy, which is in southern Brittany. We had enjoyed holidays previously in this area, where the countryside has many forests, rolling pastures and varied coastlines, some of which are very rugged and quite spectacular. The advantages of this area to us included its nearness to the north western ferry ports of France, reducing the distance to travel after leaving the boat.

On this holiday we had decided we would look for a house, which we liked and could afford to renovate, with some land, but not too isolated because we wanted to integrate into a local community.

We made our way to the small town of Baud, which reminded me of a market town in the UK. The buildings were old but all well preserved. In the lower part of the town there was a large fountain the water of which is reputed to have healing properties. Baud lies between Pontivy and Auray, surrounded by countryside through which flow the Blavet and Evel rivers. Just south of Baud are the forests of Camors and Floranges that are ideal for long peaceful walks amongst the wild life. We were surprised to find red squirrels had survived in that area and had not been driven out by the grey squirrels.

Our intention was to look at properties suitable for a holiday home. We invited Fran and Dee to join us in the gîte where we were staying and to ask for their advice on what to look for when buying property in France. In our efforts to find a suitable house, we called at the local Notaire office in Baud. Luckily for us he spoke English. He was a quaint little man with small round spectacles over which he peered when he addressed us. We were asked to sit down and were then presented with several books containing pictures and details of various properties for sale (A Vendre), in the area. We looked carefully at what was on offer and made arrangements to visit some properties during our stay. The houses we looked at on the next day, were not suitable- one was very isolated and required considerable renovation to the roof which was falling in and the walls looking insecure. The second property was a rather weird old house, dark inside and fully furnished with contents included in the asking price. In the main salon, the table had been laid as if a meal was about to be served, creating the impression that the occupants were about to appear, with spectacles beside one plate and an opened newspaper beside another. At the sides of the inglenook fireplace were two ancient wooden benches and a discarded shoe. A film of dust lay over everything with cobwebs trailing from the woodworm infested old beams. When we left this room, we followed our guide upstairs and this was worse since in the main bedroom was a large four-poster, made up with bedclothes and in the centre was a hump, looking just as if someone was still lying there. I think the agent read my thoughts and said "no problem it is empty" laughingly I replied " thank goodness". We had no hesitation in crossing this one off our list. The following day we looked over a house in a hamlet not far from Baud called Nennec. The house was not large but it had three rooms downstairs and a granary on the first floor which could be converted into two bedrooms and a bathroom. The roof was intact and the building was in a good state of repair. The walls inside all required decorating. The floors downstairs were tiled, except for a small area in the main room which was a wooden floor. The garden was half an acre which was about the size we would choose although this was entirely at the front of the property which did not allow for any privacy for sitting out in the evenings. Another drawback was the shared driveway with the next door neighbour being the only access to the house. We had recently had an unpleasant experience with a neighbour where we had a shared driveway in England. This manifested itself with the lady of the neighbour's house continually raking the new gravel we had laid, onto her side of the drive and objecting loudly to our visitors parking on it. Also her every day routine of dusting the outside of their garage door left me in no doubt that the problem was not entirely with us.

However, the price for this house in Nennec was right and it was in a good rural area of the Blavet valley, so we decided to go ahead and buy it returning to the Notaire's office the following day to complete the necessary paperwork. We signed what we thought was an agreement by the vendor to sell and an agreement that we would buy the property. We did not realise at this stage that all the vendors had not agreed to sign their part to the sale.

On our return to England we went to the building society and arranged for a deposit to be available when required. The house we wished to purchase had been left to the five children of the deceased owner of the property. Four of the children had signed their agreement to the sale but the fifth son decided to purchase the property for himself. We were very disappointed when we realised the property was not to be ours. The Notaire's wife was not best pleased, as she had taken many people to see this property. Still as my dear mother always said it was not meant to be. We had learnt a salutary lesson - the piece of paper we had signed was only our promise to buy and not a mutually binding contract.

Two years later and a little wiser I had been attending French lessons each week in the hope I would be able to converse better on our next visit. The French I had learnt at school seemed to have totally escaped me. The pound at this time was worth more francs, 9.5 francs to the pound and increasing against 7.5 francs when we were about to buy the Nennec property. We convinced ourselves that our failure to buy the property in the Blavet Valley, had been a lucky escape for us.

When we again set off to France in search of a house in February, it had not occurred to either my husband or myself that the sea on the ferry crossing may be rough. Neither of us had any tablets to take to prevent seasickness. We left Worcester at 6 am and arrived in Plymouth for the 11 a.m. boat to France. We had come well prepared for our trip with picnic basket, food in the cold box and our usual supplies of tea and coffee.

Prior to our trip we had contacted an agent in London who had put us in touch with English agents in the Morbihan area. This area is in the southern part of Brittany and the word Morbihan is a Breton name meaning little sea. It has a very large population of seabirds and a great variety of other wildlife. The climate is very mild and some Mediterranean type vegetation is found in abundance in this area. The coastline is varied with rugged cliffs and quiet sunny coves, the beaches are long and golden and dotted around can be found rock pools which are full of surprises. There are many small islands to explore and it is a land for the boat enthusiast and the fishermen.

We were due to meet up with the agents the evening of our arrival at 9.30-pm French time and they had arranged overnight accommodation for our first night in France. It was planned that they would show us some properties in the region of Morbihan. The day we crossed on the ferry was sunny but the white horses were showing on the waves as we left the harbour. We went up on deck but decided it was too chilly to remain and so we went below and bought coffee and sandwiches. Afterwards we visited the duty free shop as I had promised to buy son Richard some tobacco and my daughter Ruth some perfume.

We had been sailing for about one hour and the boat was beginning to toss around and I was beginning to feel a little queasy, when my husband said" I don't understand you, it is perfectly OK - just a bit choppy". I then recalled how a friend of ours said take ginger if you feel sea sick - ginger biscuit, ginger cake, anything with ginger in it. Luckily I had some ginger biscuits in our bag so I quickly demolished half the packet. I suppose they did some good since I did not actually vomit but I sure felt as if I was about to. The journey to Roscoff took 9 hours. We were over 1 hour late and I have never ever been so pleased to reach terra firma.

We set off from the port for Baud but with the heavy, driving rain and the darkness we managed to take a wrong turn and instead of going south we were heading north. When we realised our mistake, we had been travelling for about half an hour in the wrong direction. However we stopped, looked at the map and set forth again and without any more disasters headed for Baud. We arrived at our destination very late, just before midnight, but fortunately for us, the agents worked from home and were still up and I had a sneaky feeling they had experienced this problem with other potential house buyers. We apologised and the man of the house said he would take us to where we would be staying for the night. The man went back into the house to collect his coat and when he reappeared he was wearing a sheepskin coat, which reminded me immediately of my uncle's coat - obviously we gave him the benefit of the doubt and called it a coincidence. Back in the car we followed him for what seemed miles. When we reached our destination, it was pitch black, no street lights there. He went ahead and shouted to us" do you have a torch" "everything but" I said. "Follow me please" he said " but be careful you don't fall" We followed him up some winding stone steps without a handrail and on the outside of a tall building. Finally, we reached a door, which he opened and showed us to where we would stay for the night. The room was large and warm. We bid our farewells and said we would meet up the following morning around 10am at their office - if we could find it. There was a shower room attached to our bedroom but no facilities to make a drink. By this time we were so shattered, all we wanted was to sleep. The hard French bed had a cylindrical bolster instead of the pillows we English are so used to - but this didn't bother us - we must have been tired!

Chapter Two

Buying the House

We awoke the next morning early to find the sun was shining and the misery of the previous day was forgotten. " What do we do about breakfast?" said Les and I suggested that we went into Baud and bought coffee and a couple of croissants. We showered and attempted to dry ourselves on some frilly towelling assuming perhaps, that this was a local type of towel It was only when my husband commented on them I realised, on closer scrutiny, we had been wiping ourselves on towelling curtains.

We packed our over-night luggage into the car and drove into Baud. We found a busy little bar packed with early morning continental breakfast participants and in our best french asked for deux grande café, avec du lait et deux croissant. The lady behind the bar greeted us warmly and much to our surprise, most of the customers came and shook our hands - possibly a case of mistaken identity we assumed. At the point of our departure we perhaps over did it a little by again shaking everyone by the hand – much to his or her amusement. Our plan for the morning was to meet Silvia, the estate agent and our guide for the day. We offered to pay her for the previous night's accommodation. She asked us why we had not paid the lady at breakfast. We looked blank because we had not seen any one at the house. It had seemed to be completely deserted, except for a big life sized weird looking doll that was sat on a chair outside our bedroom door. In the dim light of the night we had arrived, it had given me a real turn. It had improved a little viewed in the daylight. Silvia said " did my husband not tell you about breakfast - you go downstairs and the dining room is inside the main doors" " Not to worry" we said, not wishing to get her husband into trouble who had not explained this. We paid the 250 francs for the night and we said we would be booking into a hotel for the next five nights. Silvia asked us into her office to complete a few preliminaries before we set off to view properties she had on her books. She produced a piece of paper which she asked us to sign." What is this?" my husband asked. "Oh, it is just to say that I have taken you to these properties". "But we haven't seen them yet" he said. I thought that Leslie was going to be difficult. My husband is an accountant by profession and I swear he does an audit on everything and the fact he was asked to sign to say he had viewed houses before he had set eyes on them, was not going to work." Oh very well" she said " sign it afterwards." Silvia then produced a list of charges, if we decided to purchase a property through them. I think it amounted to 20,000francs. "This is a bit steep," exclaimed my husband. " We have to live" retorted Silvia " so do we" said Leslie. Have you ever wished the ground would swallow you up so that you could disappear - that is just how I felt? Thankfully Silvia's husband arrived with some coffee which seemed to placate Leslie. After coffee we left in Silvia's car.

The first house we were shown was a possibility, but there was one big snag that made us cross it off the list. The location of the property was remote – in fact there was not another house in sight. Beautiful countryside surrounded the property, but since there were no near neighbours, we worried that if we bought the property, it would be empty for 70% of the year and anyone could break in undisturbed - so the answer had to be no. House number two, had a history of the English husband dying just after they bought it and it was too near to the road on a dangerous corner - not for me. Luckily Les felt the same way so we proceeded to number three. This was a very pretty cottage behind a little village church but no garden. This was not suitable as my family and I, love sitting in a garden when weather permits, so we proceeded to the next village.

As we approached house number four, there developed a strong unpleasant smell. The house was close to a local chicken rearing and processing factory. The house was a possibility but it was in the wrong position and to top it all one of the local farmers came along and disputed part of the land on the sale particulars - saying it belonged to him and was not for sale. We didn't want to get into any arguments at this stage so we made a hasty retreat. After this we returned to Sylvia's office, we bid farewell to her and said we would contact her again if we decided to pursue any of the properties to which she had taken us.

We drove into the next town of Josselin where we came across the tourist office. We enquired about accommodation or hotels in the area. They recommended a Relais hotel just outside this lovely ancient town of Josselin, which is dominated by a large magnificent chateau, called Le Château des Rohan that is still privately owned by the Rohan family. It is a remarkable mixture of feudal and renaissance architecture.

Alongside the chateau flows the wide and fast river Oust / Nantes – Brest canal.

On this particular day the chateau was reflected in the river's waters which sparkled in the afternoon sun making a lovely picture. The walls of the chateau rise sheer from the rocky river banks, culminating in three circular towers with witch-hat turrets. Beyond the forbidding exterior is a beautifully furnished interior and the ground floor is open to the public, at certain times of the year. The town has many half-timber framed houses with wooden overhangs, with tables and chairs outside the cafés in the main square. After a lengthy photographic session, we set off to look for the hotel recommended by the Office de Tourisme. Just outside of Josselin we came to a signpost showing us the direction of the hotel. We turned off the main road and followed the signs until we reached a sign saying Route Barée. The road was being made wider and resurfaced.

In my broken French I asked one of the chaps working on the road if we could go ahead but he replied " non madame- fermez". I explained we had booked at the hotel and needed to go along the road. He went and consulted with his mates and returned to tell me " keep on the left the tar is still wet " - at least that is what I think he said. At last we reached the hotel and booked in.

The receptionist asked if we wished to have a room with a balcony that was going to be extra money. As it was the middle of winter and we would be spending the daylight hours out looking at properties, we decided to forfeit the view. We were shown to our room, which was very pleasant and had en suite bath and toilet and also a balcony - was it our mispronunciation of French or was it the only room available but we did not spend time and effort in solving this mystery. We decided to book in for dinner that evening, as the menu looked enticing. The staff were friendly and I think appreciated our efforts to speak their language. We were not disappointed with the food making a mental note to eat there again. We retired after the meal, promising ourselves, an early start the next morning.

We went down to breakfast, which was the usual toasted baguettes, croissants, orange juice and choice of coffee or tea. We resisted ordering the French version of a full English breakfast.

It was very foggy outside and I thought I would be friendly with the waiter saying to Les "what is French for foggy". "I forget," said Les "look it up on your translator". I had purchased a translator in the U.K., which we found helpful on which we could get French, German, Italian and Spanish, but it was the size of a small calculator and it would not always find the words we required. However, it did translate fog as broulaide, which I pronounced as I read it. "Bon jour monsieur il est trés broulaide". He looked blankly at me as if I was a bit strange perhaps thinking "L'Anglais". I pointed at the fog and eventually he said" Oui madame broulaide" I realised it is not pronounced as it is written and he was giving us the French version.

The day turned out to be a disaster. We were to meet Maryvonne, the wife of the Notaire who was handling our previously aborted attempt to buy the house at Nennec, at the office in Baud at 10.30 am. Maryvonne was a tall good-looking woman wearing a very nice tailored suit not bought in the local marché. We were kept waiting over half an hour and when Maryvonne appeared she said that we had the wrong day. The appointment was arranged for the next day. Les hastily produced the letter we had received from the London agent spelling out the appointment time showing we were correct. She then spent a considerable amount of time in searching for her copy of the notification from the agent that she failed to find. She proceeded in an off hand manner to show us a list of properties which were all out of our price range, making our visit a complete waste of time, so we made our farewells feeling disappointed.

That afternoon we decided to visit La Baule and St Nazaire since there was little hope of making arrangements to see any more properties that day. We thought that we needed to relax and I was anxious to see how far we were from the coast. On the way we stopped at a village shop and bought some jambon, tartes pomme and of course, a baguette. We had decided we would have a picnic since the weather was warm and the sun was shining making our spirits rise. About midday we decided to stop and have our picnic. Out came the table and two chairs, which my husband insisted we bring. He said the weather would be warm and he was right. I must admit I did feel a bit conspicuous sitting by the roadside with table and chairs in the middle of February. What is it they say about mad dogs and Englishmen? I started to prepare the sandwiches and Les said he would make some tea. I love my English cuppa but somehow the French never get it quite right. We always take away with us a small Gaz primus and a kettle. "Jill where have you put the kettle" I replied "I had nothing to do with packing the kettle, Leslie - that was your job". Needless to say no kettle had been packed and the thought of a lovely English cuppa receded into the distance as we made do with lemonade, with a promise to purchase a saucepan when we came across a supermarket. You rarely see kettles in France.

We visited La Baule which reminded me of a resort on the French Riviera. The sea looked calm and blue with some children paddling in the shallows. I am sure it would be busy here in the summer with lots to do and the grand children would love it with only a short drive from the area in which we hoped to find a suitable house.

We stopped briefly at St Nazaire and shopped at the local open-air market where we bought fresh fruit. We made a mental note to return to the Ecomusée de St Nazaire where the documents of the history of the town are on show, particularly concentrating on the war time bombardments and the subsequent re-constructions. The most interesting part of the museum is apparently the submarine pens that are covered locks, which enabled German U boats to slip out of the harbour undetected.

We returned to the hotel to get ready for our evening meal. Les decided on veal and I thought I would have lamb. With our main course decided, we looked at the starters. Thank goodness for the French lessons, which were earning their keep - at least that is what I thought. Les chose the egg mayonnaise and I had chosen what I had believed to be cold boiled ham - a big mistake. Les said" you are not going to eat that are you - shall we do a swop" Please" I said (French still not good enough) The ham was virtually uncooked.

The next day was Wednesday and we were due to meet a new agent in Josselin with the purpose of visiting some more properties in the area. We arrived on time for our appointment and after a few pleasantries with the receptionist, we met Angelina who spoke reasonably good English. She was tall and slim with pretty long curly hair and bright blue eyes. She offered us coffee which I declined as usual fearing the small cups of thick black very strong substance, which is my prescription for a migraine. Her office was modern, light and airy situated on the ground floor of an impressive old building in the shadow of the famous chateau. In the course of our conversation, she informed us she had stayed for two weeks in Rugeley that is not far from Birmingham. As is customary we were given large books containing photographs and particulars of houses for sale from which we choose four and decided to proceed with the viewing. " Oh just one moment" Angelina said" I have another property which has just come into the office this morning, but there is no photograph to show you but you may wish to trust my judgement since I know the property which is in a very pretty location". We agreed to add it to our list for viewing and proceeded to squeeze into her tiny car. After leaving Josselin we travelled along various country roads for about 8 miles arriving at a small hamlet called Quelneuc, having a large farm and about twenty houses. There was one road leading through the hamlet down to a large lake and the property we were to view was the last house on this road before the lake. The house was a two hundred-year-old stone farmhouse with about 4000 square metres of land. We could see that it had been recently re - roofed with modern slates although the original ridge tiles had been used. On the first floor we noted that there was a full height granary oak door at the front and one at the rear. This indicated that the walls were sufficiently high to enable the upstairs granary to be converted to bedrooms. White shutters were fitted to the ground floor windows and the back door. We entered through the back door, which was painted bright turquoise. The first thing I noticed inside the house were the old beams and the large fireplace with little wooden benches either side of it.

The lake named Lac au Duc

House before renovation

I imagined little children sitting on them warming their toes in front of the open fire. I liked it immediately, as did my husband. This room was large with a welcoming feel about it probably due to its polished beech floor. The room was dusty with cobwebs hanging from beams infested with woodworm. I said, " I could do wonders with a paint brush here". " I think it will need a little more than a coat of paint" my husband retorted. We proceeded to look around the other room. There was a bathroom, which was on the ground floor consisting of a bath, shower, washbasin, bidet and toilet. By the appearance of the bathroom it had been installed recently. The suite was a sand colour and the walls had all been tiled with grey tiles and the floor had large brown colour tiles. Not my choice for a colour scheme but there was a basis from which things could be improved. We continued through another door and what we saw was not so good. Nothing had been done with this room which looked as if it may have been used for storage of wine. There were also several large iron rings fastened to the wall, which had been used at some time to tether animals. This area would make an ideal kitchen I decided when we had put a floor in it and plastered the walls. At the moment the floor was just earth that had been hardened over the years. We found out later from a neighbour, who had lived in the house as a child, that cattle had been kept in there. From this room we looked into the granary above from the second or third step of a very unsafe looking homemade ladder. This area would make four good-sized bedrooms, with separate toilet wash basin and shower we decided. "Let's look outside and take some photographs" I said to Les. "Angelina, how much of the land is ours" I asked as a piece of wire seemed to form the barrier." your ground covers 3,750 square metres which is roughly a quarter of a kilometre in a straight line" she said. "Who will look after all this land?" I said. " Don't worry," said Angelina " the cows will keep the grass short - they are doing it at the moment." Angelina explained that we could let the land to the farmer next door if we wished and we were advised later to consult with the land surveyor when we moved in and to get the land marked out and fenced properly.

After taking the photographs we left Quelneuc to look at more houses but I think our minds were made up - we liked the first one we had seen that day. Angelina was delighted that we had chosen the one she liked. "You can tell my boss when you see him tomorrow," she said. As we left Angelina said " can you see the lake over there - in the summer you can swim in it and the local folk also fish and they catch some grand Pêche. The lake is some 8 miles long or did she say 8 kilometres.

The next day we had arranged to go to Malestroit to meet the person who owned the agency who was Angelina's boss. Bertrand was a very friendly and helpful young man who was very easy to talk to. He had a jolly round face, curly fair hair, not in the least like a Frenchman and his English was excellent. We explained that we liked the property in Quelneuc but he said as we were there, we should visit the ones he had arranged for us to see before we made our final decision. Bertrand offered to drive us to see the properties but Les, remembering the cramped conditions in Angelina's car, insisted he would take our car" just as you like" said Bertrand "it is unusual for the English clients to drive". We set off and Bertrand was very talkative when we complimented him on his command of the English language. He asked us what part of England we came from. We explained it was near the Malvern Hills " ah!" exclaimed Bertrand "that is were the Malvern spring water comes from". " That's what you think" says Les "we just get it out of the tap put it in a bottle and then sell it to the French,"" ah! Well" said Bertrand "I will not tell you what we put in our Perrier water which we sell to the English" We burst out laughing.

We visited two houses but they were not as suitable as the one at Quelneuc and we decided to buy that one. Bertrand thought we had made the right choice. He said " it is a good property good value for money and in a very nice position". "I have enjoyed the day with both of you" he said "the driver was very good even if the traffic looked a little close on my side at times". Bertrand said that we would return to his office via Rochfort en Terre which was an award winning town of beauty and character. It only has a population of around 600 and its past has a colourful history with many impressive town houses dating back to the sixteenth century and has one of the most beautiful churches in the region. We were told that many artists and craftsmen had set up here. I would have loved to browse round the many shops - perhaps some other time. After leaving Bertrand we went back to the office in Josselin to collect the key for the house we had decided to buy, since it was empty.

The next day we went to the house to take measurements for curtains and for drawing up plans needed to start any renovation work. Les said we should open a French bank account, which would come in useful, when we wanted to purchase the house. We drove into Ploërmel, which was the nearest town to the hamlet where the house was. We found one of the national banks in the centre of the town and went inside. Speaking to the young man on reception, who I might add did not speak a word of English, we said that we wished to open a joint account but we could not find the word in French for joint account. We all started to giggle and the chap disappeared coming back with another young man. During his absence I unsuccessfully referred to my dictionary but we still were unable to get any further. The second young man did not speak English either and by this time we were at the head of a large queue. Eventually we were shown into an office, where we were greeted cordially by an older man, who did speak a little English. We explained, as best we could, that we wished to open a bank account in order to buy a property in the area. We proceeded to show him a picture of the house and on reflection, we think he thought we wanted to borrow money. When we eventually convinced him that we did not want money but to open a joint account to put money in, he became all smiles. Then we had to fill in the forms - what a fiasco - I did not realise how much importance is given to a lady's maiden name in France. After trying for another half-hour, with the help of the dictionary, I understood - je compris - and after a good deal of hand shaking, we departed.

That evening we went out to celebrate and the meal was super. We had langoustines for starters, followed by fillet steak, a selection of vegetables and a wonderful creme brulée for sweet.

Next day, we visited our house to be and found that we were only five minutes walk from the lakeside. Further round the lake there was a man made beach and a golf club with a yacht club at the far end of it - not bad eh! We went inside the house and carefully took the measurements of the walls, measured for curtains and in the process of doing this; the lady from the next house came round and introduced herself. She very kindly offered us coffee, which we readily accepted saying in our halting French, that we would come in when we had finished measuring. The lady's name was Yvonne and I judged her to be in her late sixties, very small in stature but sturdy. Her hair had been black but was now peppered with white. It was her lovely complexion that fascinated me. Her cheeks were truly rosy and weathered by the elements and I remember, despite the cool wind her sleeves were rolled up to her elbows, which we were to find in the future, was always the case. She wore only slippers with stockings hanging at half-mast above them. When we had finished measuring up we knocked on Yvonne's door and she invited us into her kitchen. In the centre of the room there was a large scrubbed table, either side of which were placed benches, where we were asked to take a seat. I foolishly sat on the end of the bench and it tipped and I nearly went flying - that was a good start. In the corner was a brick built fireplace with an open fire on which was a pot, the contents of which smelt very good and I think it was lunch cooking. The water for the coffee came in a pan from the fireplace and this was poured into a coffee jug from which she produced the coffee, which was extremely strong, and thank goodness they were only small cups.

The only other furniture was a grandfather clock, a small dresser and a television set. There were no comfortable chairs and the room was very Spartan. We learnt from Yvonne that her son owned the land round about. He was the farmer who had taken the farm over when her husband, his father, had died. She also had two daughters and several grandchildren. We explained that we wanted to buy the house for holidays at which she replied." oh, mais oui la maison trés grande pour vacance." I laughed and explained we had lots of grand children who would soon fill it up. Despite the continual heavy rain whilst we were there, causing a muddy surrounding area through which we struggled to reach our car, our enthusiasm to buy the house was not dampened. We made our farewells, feeling that this lady had done her best to welcome us to Quelneuc and we thought how lucky we would be to have her as a neighbour. How right this proved to be. We returned the key to the agent's office and proceeded to the hotel to pack because we would be making an early start back to England the next day.

Our journey back to the boat was less complicated than our outward journey and the day was sunny. We sailed at 11a.m. from St Malo since the Roscoff ferry could not sail due to the bad weather and arrived Plymouth at 7 pm - don't ask about the crossing - it was horrendous. I was seasick all the way; the winds were gale force. " I shall go by the tunnel next time" I declared. As I lay groaning in the cabin, Les arrives after having consumed a fried breakfast and not feeling any the worse for it asking if I had the measurements of the rooms and windows which we took yesterday. We thought they must be in the car. We couldn't look for them as no one is allowed on the car deck once the boat is underway. When we arrived at Plymouth, we looked in the car for the measurements. They were nowhere to be found. To put it mildly, Les was not a happy chap. What would we do now without the measurements? Where could they be? We were soon to find out.

Chapter Three

Renovating without a Toilet

We had been home a couple of days when I collected the developed photographs of the house we were buying in France. Much to our disappointment the ones I had taken outside were under exposed but the photographs I had taken of the inside of the house were clear. Guess what? The notebook, which had the measurements in, was on the windowsill for all to see, in the photograph of the main room. Les decided he would ring Bertrand and ask him if he could possibly collect the notebook and send it on to us by post. We sent the deposit for the purchase of the house in April and we waited for word to say completion was on the way. The contract for buying the property was signed in May. In the meantime Les had contacted some of our friends to ask them if they would be interested in coming to France to help renovate this old farmhouse we had bought. They were all so enthusiastic at being asked that it was decided that we would commence the renovation project in June. Les considered who he needed to take with him. He decided that he would require an electrician and Fran's son, Peter, would probably be available. He had lived in France and could speak French and was an electrician as well as a plumber. Peter was contacted and he said he would be willing to go. Les needed someone who knew about building. Robert a friend of ours would be able to do the work as he was a retired builder and also visited France regularly. He had done work on properties in France before and he could help put in the staircase we had bought in the UK. Another suitable person was Martin who was also an electrician and keen to come having taken early retirement. Now that Les had decided on his team, he had to plan the first stage of work to be done, collect the necessary equipment and tools and book the boat for the 14 June 98.

Les rang Bertrand and asked if, when we had completed the acquisition, would he make arrangements for someone to sand blast and treat the beams and any other infested wood before the visit, as he had suggested to us when we went to his office. In particular, the 15 old beams forming the ceiling downstairs needed to be cleaned and brought back to their original colour and surface. The sandblasting price included treatment of the later to be discarded, upstairs floor and the scrap wood stored on it. This was our first costly waste of money.

Bertrand agreed that he would send us our notebook with the measurements, which we had left, at the house. When we received the measurements we ordered a staircase to suit the height of the downstairs ceiling from a UK supplier since we had no idea what was available in France for this purpose. I had a tow bar fitted to my car so that we could use my son's trailer to carry tools, the staircase, four single beds and a cement mixer.

Quite a few changes had taken place since our first plan of action including the inability of Martin to come with us because he had developed a trigger finger, so it was essential that we found a replacement quickly. Ray, who had done jobs for us in the past, agreed to come. He was a good worker but he did not possess a passport and time was getting short (8 days before they were due to leave). I collected a passport application form from the post office for Ray to complete. When filling in the passport request form, there is a question, which asks if you have been called by any other name and this is where a complication arose. The surname on Ray's birth certificate was not the surname by which Ray has always been known. His mother remarried and he has always used her second husband's surname. He could not remember his name being changed officially, so we needed to consult a solicitor and sign up the necessary papers so that he could have his present name on his passport. By this time we could not chance posting the passport request because time was too short and we may not have received it back in time for their journey on 14 June 1998. We decided to apply in person to the passport office in Newport in Wales. Success at last - we managed to get the passport without any further problems after 4-hour delay. By Saturday they were all ready to leave, after some changes for example, not taking the cement mixer but innumerable tools, food to feed an army. Les, Rob, Peter and Ray arranged to depart on the Sunday at 2 pm. Ray arrived earlier than the others to give Les a hand to load the trailer. Luckily Dave, another friend of Les, came round with some lorry straps to help secure the load. We had lunch and they prepared themselves for departure. I prayed they would reach Portsmouth without mishap. As they were about to leave, Rob said "hang on - I hope you have put extra air in the tyres" "no, air is only put in when I have it serviced" I replied. " Well I suggest we get a foot pump and check the pressures because with such a load the tyres must be well inflated," said Robert. The big problem was that the foot pump was at the bottom of the fully and carefully packed boot. Already, they were 45 minutes late in departing. Luckily Sarah (Peter's sister) arrived with her boyfriend, to see her brother off. Her boyfriend said that he had a pump in his car and offered to get it. With tyres inflated - they departed. Alas, after 100 yards - they stopped. One of the straps was flapping and Rob got out to adjust it and also raise the trailer jockey wheel, which was catching on the road. They finally departed, with Les at the controls.

I received a telephone call from Portsmouth saying that they had arrived safely and were in the queue for the boat. They decided that Rob will be driver when they got to France and Les will act as navigator. I hoped for a phone call the next day saying they have arrived in Quelneuc. On Tuesday 16 June, I received a call from Les to tell me that they had arrived safely, but on the journey he did the very same thing that we did when we went over to France earlier in the year. He again took the wrong turn and was heading back towards Alençon and not Ploërmel. Eventually they proceeded on the right track. I dare not ask how they turned the trailer round. Having arrived at their destination just after lunchtime, the trailer was disconnected and left at the house in the process of going out to find food. The only place open seemed to be the most expensive place in the town. They ordered from the a la carte menu although some of them did not know what would appear on their plates. Ray, who only seems to eat chips and sausage with the occasional egg, ordered this but the chips were not like English ones and the sausage was spicy and contained almost uncooked meat. He did however drink the Coca-Cola. The others were only marginally more successful but the wine was somewhat compensating. On the way back to the house they decided that they would need a table and some chairs. This was quickly resolved by buying plastic garden furniture. The trailer and roof rack were eventually unpacked and the stairs placed in their approximate location.

Next day the stairs were fixed, but only after Les had a sleepless night pondering about their correct position. Les decided that two steps had to be taken off the bottom to get the angle of ascendancy right and the cutting out of landing points from two of the beams for securing the top of the stairs. Unfortunately, when they examined the floorboards upstairs they were found to be rotten on their upper surfaces although they had appeared sound on the undersides and had to be replaced. This entailed forming a framework above the downstairs ceiling beams because they were so old and distorted that if the framework had not been put over them, the floor upstairs would have been very uneven. This was a blow because it would delay putting the plasterboard up to form the walls of the bedrooms. The rotten wood was very kindly taken away by the farmer, Yvonne's son René, in his trailer. He also cut down the upstairs beams with his chain saw which was necessary since it would have been too big a task to cut them with handsaws. He then cut the removed beams into manageable lengths to remove from the upstairs of the house and took them away in his trailer. These beams had to be removed in order to have the bedrooms ceilings at a height where we did not have to be ducking our heads every time we entered the bedrooms, as was the case in many of the converted granary areas we had seen in France. In order to remove these beams which were supporting the main rafters of the roof we had to fix replacement timbers above them and then bolt these into the rafters to support the roof and prevent it moving from the tops of the walls. Les had problems because he was unable to find the right size bolts to secure these timbers to the main rafters and this was solved by buying metre lengths of threaded bar with nuts and tooth washers. Fortunately Les had many suitable washers which he had taken over to France left from his washer manufacturing business which he had sold in the U.K.

Les said the neighbour, Yvonne had been most helpful giving them both coffee and wine. No wonder Les sounded full of the joys of spring on the telephone, I am sure the vin rouge had been in plentiful supply. The work was heavy and the weather was beautiful for lazing on the beach but for hard work, it was very tiring. On the third day when digging out for the drains for the new toilet upstairs and the kitchen sink, it was found that some of the existing pipework to the fosse septique was cracked and leaking and the fosse was overflowing. This was not a healthy sight and attention to it had to take priority. René again came to the rescue by organising the right person to come and empty the fosse. Prior to this the toilet and washing facilities had been out of bounds until the fosse had been emptied. You can imagine how difficult the situation was and the alternatives were a visit to the surrounding fields or one of the local bars.

When the fosse was again operational, relief was expressed by all.

Les and Peter went off to buy the wood for the floorboards upstairs on which Peter was able to negotiate a good price for some reason. They also bought timber for the replacement of the beams removed. The lads worked very hard and soon in a matter of days, half the granary floor was looking like a ballroom - all we needed was Mike and his band. Mike is my music teacher who amongst other things is the musical director for a local jazz orchestra. When the floor upstairs was nearly completed, Les decided because time was getting short, the concrete for the kitchen floor should be purchased. Because our trailer was so full when they left home, they were unable to take the concrete mixer, so Les had to buy ready mixed concrete. Now how in the world was he going to explain, in French, what concrete he wanted, of the right mix, of the right amount and on top of all this get it delivered to the right place, at the right time. Out came the well-worn dictionary, which he admitted was not that good for building terms. He found a supplier who sold ready mixed concrete and asked in French for 2 cubic metres of concrete suitable for a kitchen floor. It arrived in minutes of the appointed time it was poured into the kitchen via the kitchen window, with all hands on deck the concrete was spread in about one and half hours.

The wiring in the house was very old and suspect and dangerous so Peter set about replacing the old wiring downstairs, with a temporary electrical supply. The end result of this resembled a badly planned Christmas decoration project with lights, sockets and cable hanging everywhere. Les said, " well lads wait until the wife sees this".

Sleeping arrangements were primitive to say the least but the lads had taken four single beds with them. I had bought four plastic covers for the beds since I was worried that the beds would get wet in transit. I explained to Les that the sheets were fitted sheets and the duvet covers were already on the duvets so bed making would be easy. However, the first night when they all retired there was much laughter because no one had taken the plastic covers off. When they got into bed the elastic fitted sheets went ping and by the morning they were all sleeping on the plastic and with the weather so hot you can just imagine the sweating. They removed the plastic the second night but again they had just settled down to sleep when a loud whirring was heard " I recognise that," said Robert "that's a hornet and we don't want to be stung by it". Peter quickly got out of bed and found a Vapona spray, which had been left in the bathroom, and he managed to squirt it on the offending hornet, thinking it would finish it off. This spray however, had the opposite effect causing the insect to accelerate around the room, much to everyone's dismay. Eventually Peter managed to kill it, by swatting it hard, to everyone's relief.

Food- glorious food - was a hit or a miss. Peter did most of the cooking which was quite good although some meals had to be taken at the local bistro. Facilities were a bit primitive at the house as far as cooking was concerned with only a small electric cooker, consisting of two hot plates and a small oven. They did take a slow cooker but they did not make much use of it. Washing up must have been a sight to behold particularly when the fosse was out of action. It had to be done in a bowl in the bathroom in the wash basin prior to disposing of the wastewater in the garden. There was no hot water in the sink in the bathroom because Peter was still working on the electrics. As yet the French plumber had not installed the kitchen sink when again they found that the fosse septique was overflowing which again caused an embargo to be placed on the use of the one and only toilet. I will not go into details of the alternative arrangements, which were used - I leave this to your imagination.

The access to the first floor granary was by means of the very old and woodworm infested, home made ladder - possibly around since the French Revolution.

Les needed to examine the state of the timber roof structure and floorboards in the granary at a time before he had lost two stone in weight. The result of this was that the rungs of the ladder were set free, by the two side timbers parting company, under his weight.

Fortunately for him and unfortunately for Ray who was passing underneath and cushioned Leslie's fall.

The two houses next door were on the market and we had approached Bertrand with the thought of buying them, but we were told they had been sold. However, the people buying them, were unable to obtain a mortgage. Bertrand had written to us in June to ask if we were still interested in buying the houses, as they were now back on the market. When Les reached France, he telephoned Bertrand for the keys and went to look at the properties. They needed much more in the way of renovation than the first house, which we had named Pré du Lac since it was close to the lake. After discussion we decided to buy the other houses. We had in mind turning them into two gîtes as the properties formed two houses but would need the building of a concrete partition wall from the ground level up through the joint granary to the apex of the roof. Like the first property, the roofs were new and the walls of one house had been properly pointed back. The only thought I had in mind was what would we do with all the land. "Don't worry," says Les " we will let it to the farmer". I had visions of mowing acres of grass with my push mower and the only answer is a sit on mower if René, the farmer does not wish to lease it from us.

My daughter Ruth and her two daughters arrived at our house in the UK on the Wednesday evening after I had received the phone call from Les. When I told her Les had put in an offer to buy the two houses next door to Pré Du Lac." you must be mad - what are you going to do with three houses" exclaimed Ruth. I replied that we had several options such as doing them up and selling them again with the hope of making a profit or turning them into gîtes. The latter would be a good proposition if we could let them. That was a long way off however, with months of hard work and planning but we were all very enthusiastic.

When the guys returned from France, they certainly looked tanned but exhausted. It was our aim to return in August but this time there would be Les me and Robert and his wife Ann who I had known for many years since we had worked for the same health authority. Ann was accustomed to renovating old property and she was not worried about the thought of roughing it. Our plan of action this time was to put the room partitions up on the first floor, which would allow for four bedrooms and a room with shower, toilet and wash basin. This time we would be taking the trailer laden with an old three piece suite, chest of drawers, washing machine, fridge and other small items e.g. crockery small table and clothing. Les had tried to book the Portsmouth to St Malo crossing but it was full and eventually we managed to get a place on the Poole to Cherbourg during the day. The crossing was only four and a half hours but it did of course, mean more driving when we reached France. However, we booked the Ferry for the 6 August 1998.

The departure day was rapidly approaching and there were many things to get ready. Whilst the men would be busy occupying themselves with room dividers, Ann and myself would be hell bent on getting the place cleaned up. I wanted to hire an industrial hoover when we arrived but my dear husband said that there was no need. There is only some dust in the fireplace, which he forgot to move. However, we will wait until we get there. It never ceases to amaze me how men always fail to see dust or dirt anywhere.

CHAPTER FOUR

Topless near St Nazaire

The day of my first visit as property owner dawned and I was wondering whether we had taken on more than we had bargained for but the weather was dry and sunny. My spirits began to rise as we started our new route down to Poole. The journey was uneventful with our furniture and kitchen appliances remaining in place on the trailer. It took three hours to reach the boat and the crossing was smooth taking another four hours. After having our lunch in the boat cafeteria, we sat out on deck for most of the crossing, which turned out to be quite eventful and entertaining. We had left Poole about two hours, settled ourselves down to do a little serious sunbathing, when a helicopter appeared above us. It circled round the boat, soared up into the blue sky and made a nosedive towards the sea. Just above the water it pulled out of the dive and flew off into the distance. It subsequently re-appeared and repeated the exercise. We were not sure what they were trying to prove but it certainly left us quite astonished, wondering if it was an emergency or just a practice for one. However we reached Cherbourg on time and commenced the long drive down the peninsular to Dinan and then on to Quelneuc.

Robert, Les and I shared the driving and despite the roadworks, we arrived at our destination in about five hours. We did stop at one of the table and chairs picnic areas commonly found by the side of French roads. We had slightly stale sandwiches with yogurt and fruit, which I had packed the previous day. I must say we were hungry by this time.

When we reached Quelneuc we were made welcome by the neighbour's dog Belle. She had remembered Les from the previous visit. She was a strange looking dog resembling a fox with lovely golden eyes. She did not make friends readily and had to get to know you but it helped to have a few tit bits on hand to give to her. In time she allowed me to stroke her and we eventually became the best of friends. Often, when I took a walk down to the lake, she would appear at my side to accompany me. Yvonne told me that Belle had never done this with anyone before. She had always been a working dog who had been trained to round up and take the cows to the milking shed accompanied by the farmer, René on his two stroke motor bike. René placed blue string across our driveways to fool the cows into believing that it was the electric fencing. The neighbours, Yvonne and any of us who might be around armed with sticks, were posted along the route to keep the cows on track.

When we opened the front door we were overwhelmed with the awful smell of sewerage and the place had dust everywhere from the sand blasting of the beams and other woodwork. The bathroom was a sight to behold - with mud on the floor tiles and the debris from the removed upstairs floorboards, which had fallen into the bath, washbasin and bidet. Where would we start? "Les, where is this smell coming from" I asked. Robert said, "run the taps the traps must have dried out." We ran the taps and sure enough the smell began to fade, but we found the waste pipe for the new kitchen sink had not been connected, with the result that all the fumes from the septic tank were coming up the pipe into the kitchen. Robert sealed the pipe end with plastic, which temporarily solved the problem. We opened all windows and doors and set to cleaning. Ann grabbed a broom to sweep up the sand blast dust. I had brought some Domestos to clean the bathroom remembering to avoid it going down into the septic tank. All the chaps could think of, was when were they going to eat, but the preparation of the food had to wait until we had made the bathroom and kitchen area reasonably clean and within a couple of hours that was done. With all the floors swept, we could make up the beds and with the bathroom now clean, we could all have a shower or bath. The kitchen was really non-existent except that the floor was now concreted. The chaps unpacked the trailer and put the fridge and the washing machine into the kitchen and we proceeded to unpack them ready for use. Les, on his previous trip, had bought some worktops, which had not yet been fixed, so Ann and I proceeded to prop these up between the fridge and table to form makeshift kitchen work surfaces. I was pleased that we had invited Ann as she was a help with the decorating, cleaning and organising the kitchen I think a lot of this was down to the years she had spent in the operating theatre, as an anaesthetic sister, where organisation and cleanliness are so important.

As yet, there were no bedrooms walls- just a space where they would be eventually. Ann and Rob voted to sleep upstairs and Les and I would sleep downstairs. The weather was very hot but we all slept fitfully on our first night.

We awoke early, eager to get started and Ann and I prepared our usual breakfast of cereal and toast. After we had washed up, Ann and I set off to the town and shop for food.

On my previous visit, I had not seen much of the local scenery, so it was with surprise when, on our way to the local supermarket, we travelled on the road which wound its way along the side of the Lac au Duc.

The lake looked beautiful that morning with the sun shining on the water and the colourful sails of the small boats reflecting in the lake. The sky looked so blue, I thought it would be lovely to capture the scene on canvas. We arrived at a supermarket and I was quite pleased with myself at the amount of French I had remembered. With Ann's help, the shopping expedition went off without a hitch. In the meantime, the chaps had been busy getting timber organised with the studding for the upstairs bedroom walls and by the time we arrived back, work was going on in earnest.

Ann and I had decided that in the mornings we would have cereal toast or croissants, the odd piece of fruit or yogurt. Cooked breakfasts were not on the menu!

Lunch would be simple, mainly ham or chicken, paté, French bread of course and salad with fruit for dessert. In the evenings we would cook our main meal and this was agreed with everyone. I think the men were so pleased to think the meals would be prepared for them, unlike the previous visit when it was down to the lads themselves to do the cooking. We will not go into that, considering I found my slow cooker full of foul smelling food, which someone had forgotten to dispose of at the end of the June visit.

Mealtimes were a success because the weather was so good; all our meals were eaten outside. Just a few yards from the back door was a large bay tree from which I trimmed back the lower branches so that we were able to use its shade to sit under. On the third evening, we were so hot we decided to walk down to the lake to cool off.

At midnight, the moon was full and hung in the sky like a huge silver ball. The stars were out in force and the sky was so clear. When we reached the lake, there was a little breeze. It was a wonderful sight to see the lake shimmering in the moonlight, looking almost fairy like, reminding me of my childhood when the summer evenings always seemed warm and the stars bright. It really was a pleasant experience. The same evening we were late getting to bed, but during the early hours a dog barking disturbed me. I decided to get up and visit the bathroom, without putting on my slippers because we had swept all the floors. I walked bare foot to the bathroom. Drowsy with sleep, I put the bathroom light on and when I opened my eyes fully - wow! Large beetles everywhere and did I scream - needless to say the whole household heard about them.

We found a spray that my friend Fran had said to take with us for killing ants and cockroaches. We sprayed it all over them and this did the trick causing them to turn their toes up and enabling me to sweep them outside. Eventually, we all returned to bed but I couldn't sleep since I had visions of a beetle in the bed and I remembered seeing a film on television where a beetle crawled into someone's ear. However, they left me well alone and I slept, eventually.

The next morning I sprayed all the air vent openings into the bathroom with the insect spray, hoping this would deter our night callers. The next night I crept into the bathroom, with my shoes on and found only two beetles. These were two too many, so the next day I put Domestos down all over the floor which I diluted with some water and it did the trick - our insect visitors did not return.

Work in the kitchen was going well we plugged in the fridge, but we did not do so well with the washing machine. When we placed a load of washing in to wash, the machine started jumping all over the room. Les said that we should have removed the plate that stopped the drum moving when the washing machine is in transit, before attempting to use it. We learn something everyday.

Next morning, the local French plumber arrived. He did not speak any English, so out came the dictionary but we survived and he did a grand job removing old pipe work and installing the kitchen sink. Now we could wash up properly and no more washing up in the wash basin in the bathroom. Our next real problem was the cooker, which only had two hotplates, grill and small oven. If you put the grill on, only one of the hot plates worked so when cooking a meal it was limiting. However, we solved the problem by using the slow cooker for all the meat and cooking the vegetables on the hob.

Sunday was our day of rest so we decided to go to the coast for the day. We set off early, the sun was shining and it was already hot. We headed for La Baule and St Nazaire. In the latter, we visited a street market and we purchased some fruit and it was hot enough for me to invest in a sun hat.

We headed along the coast and found a stretch of beach, which was not crowded, and we all proceeded to get into our swim clothes. That is, except Les, who had forgotten to bring his trunks but he paddled. The water was really warm, but so was the sand, which burnt your feet as you walked through the sand dunes. I was the only one who ventured in for a swim and I found out why later. Robert was busy drawing a picture of his wife, who was topless. Poor Les did not know which side to look at first. Robert was an accomplished artist and had drawn a pencil picture of the chateau at Josselin, which now hangs on the wall in our salon.

On leaving the beach, we went on to a small walled town called Guerande. We walked round the town and had our lunch in a local Bistro that seemed to be popular and typically french. We sat outside at a table under a colourful sunshade. It was a favourite meeting place of the local people. Several of the more elderly residents were sitting at the nearby tables, enjoying their aperitif and talking happily together. How wonderful retirement can be - just doing nothing. We were told by le garçon that the temperature was 35c in the shade and 45c in the sun. I chose a lamb dish, the pronunciation of, which was difficult, but we succeeded in getting the waiter to understand us. The others all had salad dishes with seafood. We indulged ourselves in a carafe of local wine. After lunch we wandered around the mediaeval town which was completely surrounded by ramparts. It stood on a plateau overlooking the salt marshes where, from June to September the salt - pan workers harvest white table salt and coarse grey salt.

When it was time to depart, we looked at the map for a different route home. We decided to go via a town called Roche-Bernard. This ancient town is built on high ground dominating the east bank of the Vilaine estuary. In its distant past it had been an important seaport where a Norman descendant of the Vikings called Bernard had built a castle on the rocky out crop and the town gets its name from this man. Today there is a very fine suspension bridge that affords views of the valley below. The once busy commercial port is now a popular paradise for sailors with yachts and cabin cruisers. We walked through the town and stopped at a small café for some lemon tea. We sat outside in the sun looking at the charming 15th and 16th century houses. When we left the café we wandered up to a small square and admired the picturesque old town hall. We were all beginning to wilt so we decided it was time to return to Quelneuc.

The next day, Ann and I scraped the paint off the walls in the large room downstairs and when this was done, we painted on some foul smelling damp proof paint and was I glad when this job was done - it nearly anaesthetised us.

We explored the two other houses that we had purchased and concluded the work on these would take some time. The second house next door to Pré du Lac only had dirt floors in the two rooms downstairs and upstairs was a granary shared with the third house. In one room downstairs was a large inglenook type fireplace, which would have to be cleaned up because the inside of the chimneybreast, was covered in a tar like substance. I suspect that this had accumulated over many years from the remains of some animals cooked on the spit over the fire. The walls in this room were festooned with cobwebs and the crumbling plaster hung from the walls. The exposed ceiling beams were riddled with woodworm but Les was of the opinion that only two of the beams would have to be scrapped. The floorboards in the granary would all need to be replaced and the walls all needed to be re- plastered. Water at some time had been laid on and there was a sink in the far corner of the large room. We suspected that the water came from the village well. The adjoining room would make a good size kitchen and upstairs we would easily get five bedrooms in and a bath and shower room if we made a first and second floor. In the first house we only had a first floor in the existing granary. On the other two houses we would utilise the roof space to make a second floor. The back and front doors of the middle house would need to be replaced and also the woodwork round the windows needed replacing.

The third house was slightly better, with a concrete floor and a more modern stone fireplace, in the room, which would become the lounge, but not much else. The saving grace with these three houses was their refurbished roof structures, new roof tiles supported by two feet thick stone walls of some 200 years standing. The important feature was the height of the walls at the eaves, which allowed for normal height rooms on the first floor. A further building was discovered in the grounds, which was of very sound construction and would make a gîte if this was decided. We refer to it as the cave which would need to be emptied first of all the brushwood and old farm implements. We learnt from the neighbours that this building was used as the cider-making house. When we entered the cave through a very rickety door, I looked in astonishment at all the rubble. The floor was covered in debris made up with fallen stonework and old wooden beams. The walls were covered in ivy and wild honeysuckle; little lizards darted merrily about in the warm sunshine. A small owl took of noiselessly on its wings from the far corner, a tiny snake slid across the floor obviously annoyed at being disturbed. Out in the sunlight once more, I discovered in the garden a peach tree, which was full of peaches not yet ripe. A little way on from the peach tree were several walnut trees and hazelnut trees. We had not yet walked to the end of the land we own because of the farmer's cows were using it for grazing but this is a mixed blessing since they did keep the grass short.

Our stay was drawing to a close and work done had been satisfactory. Robert had nearly completed one room upstairs and the studding for the second bedroom. We now had a workable kitchen, just waiting for the floor to be tiled, the walls to be rendered and kitchen cupboards to be erected and work tops secured. In the past we talked about the furniture we would need. I had said we must get a comfortable bed and my son had suggested buying a waterbed. My son always had mad ideas. " Imagine you having one of those" my husband said " you would need to take QUELLS before you go to bed each night" I replied "now Les don't mock - you may be sea sick on one of our trips over, especially in the wintertime".

Our return journey was uneventful with a calm sea and the sun shining, arriving on time at Poole and home by lunchtime, with a feeling of satisfaction from a good start on the project.

CHAPTER FIVE

The Straw Man

In October we were preparing for our third working visit to Quelneuc. This time Les and myself would be taking Ray again who had managed to take more holiday from his permanent full time job and David, a friend of Les who fortunately worked for himself and was able to take time off to come with us when he is needed. Ray was a friend of the family. He was a small, thin, fair haired, energetic young man who was very keen to be going abroad for the second time. We would be sailing from Portsmouth to Caen; leaving Portsmouth at 7.45 am, which would mean leaving Worcester in the early hours. Ray said he would stay the night and help us load the trailer and we made arrangements for David to come round at 3.30 am. This time we would be taking the cement mixer, a three-seater settee, chests of drawers, crockery and kitchen cupboards. The plan for packing these into the trailer required a great deal of thought and ingenuity. A few days before we were due to leave, Les said that David would be coming to our house to discuss what tools would be needed and the work to be done. He arrived at 7pm as arranged. I had only met him briefly before, when he had kindly let us have some straps to help secure the trailer on their first trip to France. He is tall and slim, with a trace of red in his hair colouring and has bright alert brown eyes. He is a Scot by birth who has retained much of his Scottish accent which becomes more pronounced after having a few wee drams. On this occasion he had spent most of his day working in a barn or so we assumed from the quantity straw in his hair and on his boots and trousers. I went to make the tea and left them to talk about the arrangements for the visit to France and the discussions seemed to have been useful. David left about 10 pm but

I was worried that on Sunday he would not wake up in time so I said I would telephone him at 3am. He said that this would be fine although I did not entirely share his degree of confidence.

The day before we were leaving we packed the trailer with the help of my son Richard and Ray who came to stay that night. We retired to bed early so that we would be up at 3am ready for the drive to Portsmouth. I awoke at 3am and telephoned David who asked if he could speak with Les. I heard a few exchanges of conversation and the phone was replaced. Les came into the kitchen and said "David will not be coming since he cannot find his passport" " I don't believe it - I just don't believe it" I said. "Stop sounding like Richard Wilson" said Les. I replied " who is he supposed to be " "He is the one foot in the grave man" Les replied. I thought that this was an appropriate situation for another episode of this TV programme with someone not looking for his passport until a few minutes before he was about to leave.

We all looked disappointed and Ray was concerned because with one down the work we had planned on doing would not be achieved. "Well it can't be helped - lets get ready and set off" said Les. Just as we were going out of the door, the phone went again and it was David who had found his passport, but he was not yet fully packed. "Well hurry up "says Les "we will wait until 4am then we must go or we will miss the boat". Two minutes to four he arrived and we all set off. I might add poor David has never been allowed to forget the incident each time we go to France I say "got your passport"

We arrived in Portsmouth at 7.30 and we embarked straight away. We went into the self-service cafeteria for a breakfast of scrambled egg, bacon and thick French coffee and when we had finished David went to the duty free to buy some tobacco. We went to get some wine and chocolates to take with us, before going to find the couchettes (reclining seats). When we reached the deck where the couchettes were, we were told that a school party had reserved them for the trip so we decided to go to one of the lounges and put our feet up there. None of us had much sleep and we had hoped to sleep so that we would be refreshed for our journey from Caen to Quelneuc.

We found some bench seats and settled for a nap. At about mid- day we were all awake accept for Les who was still snoring happily - they nick named him the chain saw. We ate the picnic I had brought and it was soon 2 pm and we disembarked and commenced our journey to Quelneuc. We had a stop on the way for the necessary and a cup of coffee making good time until we reached Rennes. Les looked at the map and said, " let's try this way to Quelneuc because it will be shorter than the road we took last time". Unfortunately, it was not found straightaway and the journey turned out to be 30 miles longer.

When we arrived it was dark and whilst the lads unloaded the trailer, I prepared the evening meal as we were all hungry and thirsty by now. We opened a bottle of wine to have with our meal, which was adequate for three of us, as Ray preferred to drink Cola. After dinner I made the beds up and it was decided Ray and David would sleep upstairs where the bedrooms would be eventually and Les and I would sleep downstairs. After seeing off a few very large spiders, we all went to bed.

The following day Les went off to buy some more timber and plaster board for the upstairs room walls and I went to the local super market to buy food. That day Fran and Derek came to stay on the basis that they would bring their caravan to sleep in and have meals with us. The work on the house was going much as Les had planned it. Fortunately David and Ray got on well, working together and the working atmosphere was lively and full of fun. David named Derek ' clerk of works ' because of his custom of standing over the people working with his hands on his hips. Ray helped Les with the plaster boarding and timber for partition walls. David got on with the conversion of a large upstairs granary-loading door into a window. This door on the first floor was, in the distant past, used to transfer grain and other feed in and out. The wood still looked reasonably solid and David said he would remove all the old paint and plane the wood to smooth it and use the best of the timbers for the piece below the window. Half of the old door now became window with glass and the bottom remained wooden. When David had finished, it really looked in keeping and we could now see outside from upstairs which gave us a wonderful view of the fields, woodland and the lake in the distance.

I showed Dee and Fran around the house. She looked at me and said "all very nice with only the work now to be completed" They had done the same sort of thing with their French property, only now theirs was fully renovated and looked in character but with all modern facilities. We all enjoyed their stay with us. They had brought plenty of wine with them and I must say the meals were better washed down with good wine. We all enjoyed being together once more - like old times in the UK.

On the Thursday, Fran and Dee and I went off for the day to visit Vannes on the West Coast. This is a lovely city, built in the shape of an amphitheatre at the northern end of the Morbihan Gulf. Ramparts with a magnificent cathedral surround the old part of the city. There is a pedestrian area covering many streets, pavement cafés and high quality shops. The buildings were very old, but had been well preserved in character. As we meandered through the town we came across a market which proved to be very interesting with typically French fish stalls selling lots of unfamiliar fish. Fran and Dee said that they would like to return to be able to spend more time exploring.

At lunchtime we bought three large baguettes full of jambon and salad. We drove down to La Baule where we ate our baguettes on a bench by the sea. The sun was shining and the day was warm, tempting Dee to look at the cost of property in the area but being by the sea and in this very popular resort, it was very expensive. A flat overlooking the sea with two bedrooms, a lounge and kitchen was over £100,000 - "just hope we win the lottery" said Dee. When Dee and Fran departed on the Friday it was very quiet and we missed their company, but the work went on. On the Sunday, we had a day off and we took the lads to the coast but sod's law - it poured with rain all day. The rest, however, did them good and they were interested in the marinas and the aligned prehistoric standing stones in Carnac.

The origin of these stones is somewhat mysterious, dating back to Neolithic periods when man was developing settled communities for farming and buildings. These stones are world famous for discussions by archaelogists. Carnac is an ideal sea resort with boats, golden beaches, pine forests and oyster farming. David and Les went to look round a museum wanting to find out more about the strange standing stones whilst Ray and I stayed in the car - too tired to move.

The following morning there was some commotion outside the kitchen window and low and behold, a cow was giving birth to a calf right in front of the house. Its a good job I am a nurse and not squeamish. I called to the others to come and watch and Ray got his camera. He was clicking away as if the scene was to be made into a movie. I wondered to whom he would be showing these photographs.

In the afternoon, Yvonne called us over to the farm to watch all the tractors moving in and piling up the mounds of maize grain, used for feeding the cattle during the winter. It really was a spectacular sight to see the young men weald the tractors around up and over the mounds of grain. Afterwards, we all went into the barn joining the farmer, his family, the tractor drivers and local people for home made Calvados, cider, beer or fruit juices. It was the first time I had met René, the farmer, who was typically French in appearance with dark hair and dark laughing eyes. After being in his company for a short while, his good sense of humour came through and the family made us all very welcome. René spoke very good English but when I told him so he said " I will speak no more in English because you must learn French, in two years you will speak good French". I notice on a regular basis that he corrects my mis-pronunciations, which I now find very useful.

Our stay was drawing to a close and on the last night, we went to an Italian restaurant in Ploërmel. The Italian meal made a change from French cuisine - the wine was excellent and the staff was friendly. We ordered rice dishes but the manager came back to us with a small box in his hand saying, " this is all the rice we have left. " Les said we could have brought our own if we had known" Everyone was amused and the alternative selections were agreed. The meal progressed with many salads, pasta and cheese and amusing comments from the proprietor. Afterwards Les attempted to pay with his French credit card (which transpired to be for use only in cash machines) the owner rejected this. After further discussions, Les was getting slightly frustrated, gave the manager his AA breakdown card. The proprietor recognised what this was immediately and milked this situation by putting the AA card through his machine and in true Italian style, repeatedly rubbed the card on his trouser leg - before trying again. Eventually the Barclaycard came to the rescue to everyone's amusement and we left assuring him that we would return. He replied, wiping his brow " Oh! Mon Dieu"

On our day of departure we were up at crack of dawn to arrive at the ferry port on time. The sea trip was calm and we all arrived home - glad to be back once more needing a rest before our next visit planned for November 1998.

CHAPTER SIX

Water down the Chimney

Our next visit was later in the year than we anticipated. It was in December and the house was cold because of the wind whistling through the gaps at the eaves and through the old granary door. We only took Dave with us and the purpose of this visit was to finish more plaster boarding of the partition walls forming the other three bedrooms and shower room. Before leaving for France Les had arranged by telephone/ fax, for the French plumber to install the shower, washbasin and toilet in our absence which hopefully would be finished before our arrival.

It was very heartening to find this had been done.

When we had the necessary plasterboard in place, we asked the French electrician if he could install switches and sockets to the rooms upstairs. Our journey from the ferry had been long and tiresome, with the road continually showing the signs of ROUTE BAREE, which necessitated many detours. It must be at this time of year, that the French choose to repair the roads. We arrived home about 8pm exhausted but fortunately I had taken with us a casserole, which contained beef and vegetables, and all I had to do was to re-heat it in the microwave.

The house, this visit was much cleaner and the plumber had finished his work to our satisfaction. We now had a shower room with shower toilet and wash basin upstairs, at a plumbing and electrical installation cost of 4000 francs. We went to bed around 9 pm to make an early start the next day. The plaster boarding was erected without too many problems. However, we found that the first part of the ceiling had been put up higher than necessary. Because of this we had to buy concrete blocks and cement to fill the gap between the ceiling and the top of the walls on the whole of the first floor. This incurred extra costs because we had to put in all the ceilings to this higher level, for which we had not budgeted. We comforted ourselves by the old saying that you live and learn - we would not be making the same mistake with the other properties. Headroom is something to consider very carefully when renovating old houses.

The fireplace had not been used for many years and the bottom of the chimney had been sealed with odd bits of timber. When you looked up the chimney, it was very dirty and untidy so we decided to take all the old wood out and make two sliding panels, with handles, under the chimney opening. If in the future we wished to have an open fire we just slide the wooden panels out. These panels would prevent much cold air coming into the room.

Dave removed the rubble from the chimney that was caked with deposits from the wood and meat, which had been burnt over the many years. We decided it must be swept and asked Yvonne if she would tell the sweep for us. Two nights later it rained heavily and currently I was sleeping downstairs near the fireplace. In the middle of the night I was awakened by a noise of running water and my feet were wet. I crossed the room in the dark, to find the light switch and when the light went on, I could see that the fireplace and surrounding area was under water.

As it turned out the old timber and rubble we had removed from the chimney had been stopping the rain from coming in and our neat wooden doors were not thick enough to hold back the rainwater. Out came the buckets and odd bowl to catch the drips - apparently the seal at the top of the chimney was leaking and needed to be replaced. This was a further job, but for the moment I must relocate my bed.

The next day the rain stopped and we were busy outside moving items and tools no longer required in the first house, into the next house for storage. In the end house, Les noticed something shining in the sun in the room where we had put the concrete mixer. Thinking it was a piece of glass, did not bother to pick it up since he was waiting for an artificial hip joint and was reluctant to bend due to pain. Later on Dave said, " are finders of treasure-trove here the keepers". "Oh I should think so" said Les. Dave had seen the same shiny object as Les had and picked it up. He showed it to us and we thought it was some sort of cap badge, military in origin, gold in colour, heavy, showing an eagle with wings out stretched, perched upon a globe and above the bird was a crown. We thought it could have been German in origin from the occupation. Many nationalities had been in France in this area during the war. Not far away, is a monument in memory of the many people who had died taking part in the Second World War Resistance. We showed the badge to the French electrician who said he knew someone who might be able to tell us about our find so we gave it to him and awaited the result with interest.

In the post, before we left for France in December, we had received a letter from the Notaire. This was explaining that the Taxes Foncières (a regional tax similar to community charge here) had been paid by the previous house owner for that year and the proportion relating to our period of ownership of the house, should be refunded to Madame Ecorchard - the previous owner. She lived in Loyat - but how would we find her since in France in the rural areas with no numbers on the houses, no road names as we have in England. I decided that I would ask Yvonne if she could take me to Mde Ecochard's house. My French was improving a little but my pronunciation was poor on occasions. At times when I spoke with Yvonne, she became frustrated with my lack of comprehension but instead of speaking more slowly, she would speak more quickly and each time she repeated herself, she shouted a little louder. However, we usually eventually understood each other with the aid of a dictionary and our own sign language. I collected Yvonne and along with my husband, we set off for a neighbouring village called Loyat. We found the house without difficulty, concluding that Yvonne knew where to go. We were welcomed inside and we met Madame Ecochard and her daughter and we explained the purpose of our visit with the aid of the letter and our French / English dictionary. We were not entirely convinced that she knew why we were insistent on giving her the cheque. The mademoiselle produced her own dictionary and the situation became really funny with comparisons of the dictionaries. We were asked if we would like some vin rouge or café and we opted for the vin. Madame then appeared with some fancy snacks and our visit was most enjoyable. We paid the good lady the cheque, which she was pleased to receive and after much conversation and gesturing by all parties, we bid our farewells.

The next day we decided to give ourselves a day off and visit Auray which is on the coast, just west of Vannes. We had been told that Auray had a very large street market. The sun was shining when we set off for Auray, which we found to have interesting old sixteenth century buildings and narrow streets. After going round the market and making a few purchases, we went down to the harbour. Here we went inside a small bistro at the side of the quay and had a coffee and some French pastries. Unfortunately there was a wee dog who would insist on jumping up on my lap, much to Les's disgust although it was a change from my Siamese cat at home. We decided that when our visitors start coming to stay with us, we would bring them to Auray since it was such a quaint old town and harbour.

Time always seems to go so quickly when we are over in France. This is probably because there is always so much to do and so little time to get it all accomplished.

The evening before we were due to return to England, we went out to our little Italian restaurant for a meal where the Patron recognised us from before and he welcomed us, literally with open arms. Once again the food was excellent and plenty of it and the wine and company were good and we all slept well afterwards.

The next day we left Quelneuc early for the homeward bound ferry. The weather was foul and it was a good job we had packed most of our luggage into the car the night before. Visibility on the road was poor with lots of fog around and with the darkness, as it was only 4am, we were lucky to arrive at the port on time. Driving on the wrong side of the road in these conditions, with our headlight beam deflectors seemingly useless, it was trés difficile. When we embarked, we made a beeline for the cafeteria where we ate a hearty breakfast and after this we had a sleep for a couple of hours. The duty free shop opened about 10am, so we made a few purchases and settled down again to try and sleep. The crossing from Cherbourg to Portsmouth was calm thank goodness and from Portsmouth we had a safe journey up to Worcester.

CHAPTER SEVEN

The Dawn Patrol

Wednesday 24 February 1999 we arranged for David to come for a meal before we set off for Portsmouth to catch the 11pm boat for Cherbourg. He arrived with passport and not decorated with straw. The crossing was bearable - despite all cabins being booked but we managed to get three seats, which reclined and so we were all able to doze, some more fitfully than others. Dave disappeared during the night and we found him in the main lounge, stretched out on one of the long seats. Prior to this trip, I had purchased from Boots two wrist bands at a cost of £7.50 which were said to prevent sea sickness - when you feel sick you just press the little button on the band and within 5 minutes the sickness disappears.

I put them on my wrists and I did not feel sick at all, but the sea was very calm so perhaps conditions were not suitable for testing the wristbands.

We arrived in Cherbourg to see the sun rise and set off for Quelneuc with the weather mild and the roads quiet. From Cherbourg, the journey down the peninsular seemed long, after the restless night. We were all feeling tired when we arrived at the house around lunchtime. I had packed some food in the U.K. so we were able to eat straight away and after lunch, we all commenced working. The first job was to place all beds into the bedrooms - yippee! - We all had rooms at last. Until now, we had slept downstairs or on the landing. Poor Dave slept in a room on previous visits, with no glass in the window where he must have been freezing but he never complained. He had spent years in the army, which had prepared him well for this.

The partition walls upstairs by now were nearly complete, with just the doors to be fitted and plaster board to be put up on one of the room ceilings making all bedrooms ready for the plasterer. On our last trip, we had a leaking chimney and in our absence the roofer had repaired it, so now the inglenook fireplace was dry.

I had visions of finding the floor wet and horrid but I had a pleasant surprise. As usual, I set about cleaning. I had the distinct impression that my sole purpose in life was to be head cook - sorry correction - only cook and only cleaner but who else was capable and willing. The lounge was very dirty again where the electricians had been installing more sockets and switches in our absence. I cleaned the salon and the kitchen floors then proceeded to clean upstairs. This was difficult, in particular scrubbing the original floorboards, which needed their surfaces to be sanded because they were pitted from grain storage over the years. In the two bedrooms, on the other side of the house, the floorboards had been replaced with new ones making them easy to clean - ah well- this was a good recipe for housemaid's knee.

Les and Dave were busy finishing off plaster boarding and making more dust until 7pm. By this time, I had done as much cleaning as I could and I went down to prepare the evening meal. During each visit to France, our friends Yvonne and her son René, usually give us a bottle of home made Calvados which is much too strong for our palates, so I started using it for cooking.

We had brought some pork from home and I prepared some onion stock and garlic and placed the pork fillet in the pot, pouring over about 3 tablespoons of Calvados to tenderise the pork and placed the saucepan on the top of the cooker to simmer - French style. When it was nearly cooked, I added apple rings and with the roast potatoes and vegetables it made a very welcome meal. After the meal I washed up, whilst the men drank a night-cap or two and we all retired to our beds - absolutely exhausted.

The next day, I made the house ready for two more people I was expecting - our friends Fran and Dee. They were arriving at the weekend and I wanted to make the house show the improvements we had made since their last visit. I had brought over from England, some small mats for the floors given to me by my friend May who is always producing things for the French house. David even managed to pick some wild daffodils in the garden, so I placed them in a vase on the bedside locker to make their room look welcoming, thinking that perhaps if they looked at the flowers, they would not notice that the walls had not been plastered. My next job was to decorate the lounge and I had brought some paint from home, which was pale lemon matt emulsion. After sweeping down the walls, to make them cobweb and spider free, I proceeded to colour the walls, using sponge pads with which I could put the emulsion on thicker. It worked well and avoided the necessity for a second coat of emulsion. The salon was at last looking cleaner and more like our lounges at home. During the morning, covered in paint looking a complete mess, my friend from next door Yvonne arrives and kissed me four times. Initially you only get one kiss or perhaps two at the most and it takes time to reach four and once you do you are friends for life. I struggled with my French as usual but we were not so tense and we could laugh at my mistakes. Yvonne was pleased to see us and we had our coffee that was not up to French standard but she drank it. I decided that Yvonne must be getting used to our French pronunciation, or we were getting better, because the conversation was beginning to flow. We noted that René, her son had been building a paddock adjacent to our land, which I thought was for the cows when they were near to producing their calves. Later I learnt from René, this was used at an earlier stage in the cattle reproduction process to assist the visiting bull. I hoped that the fencing was strong enough!

On the Thursday evening, we washed and changed to go to the local bar. I cannot call it a pub in the English sense of the word, but you can buy alcoholic refreshment or coffee and also eat if you so wish. The landlady is called Mimi, which later I discovered to be the abbreviation for Maryvonne. In appearance she is short but well built, with very expressive eyes, fair hair and an outgoing bubbly personality. She speaks very good English, which no doubt she acquired when working as an international telephone operator in Paris. We believe that she gave this up to return home to run the family bar / mini market for her mother.

We quickly got to know her and she has been most helpful to us regarding our locality and introductions to people who live there and keeping us up to date on the activities within the community. Both Les and Dave had taken a shine to her - she flirts outrageously and gets away with it. We had a drink and a chat with some of the locals, but there were not many in our age group on that particular evening. Most of the people, who frequent the bar, are the young set. There were machines for playing football and various other games used for most of the evening. We bid everyone bonne nuit and forgetting to pay for our drinks set off for Ploërmel. A little way along the road I asked who had paid for the drinks and after a few moments of deadly silence, we returned to apologise and pay the bill. To our surprise, Mimi did not seem to be at all concerned but we felt that this had established our sense of fair play for which the English are noted.

We eventually arrived in Ploërmel and visited the bar, which the lads had used on their first visit, when our fosse septique had been out of action. Les was immediately recognised, for some reason and the usual custom of hand shaking followed. This bar is always busy with the attraction of satellite football, pool tables and lottery television. Les's first visit to this bar was during the world cup football tournament, during which our crew was branded jokingly as the English hooligans.

The next day I went to the local supermarket to purchase some provisions, after which I went to look at some beds since we needed to buy another single bed. We had only brought four single beds over from home and with Fran and Dee coming, we would need five. I liked the look of a pine bed in one of the local stores costing the equivalent of £75. When Les saw this he said, "this is cheap". I said "I hate to disillusion you Les, but that is just the bed base - the mattress and the head board will be more". Les said "you have got it wrong". "Would you like a bet" I said. "Accountants are not gamblers – especially when there is no chance of collecting any winnings" he said. The final price complete was over £200, but reluctantly Les made the purchase.

That night, Les said " I am sleeping on the new bed after paying all that for it" - This decision seemed to have little regard for my poor back, which ached periodically being something I had retained from years lifting patients. However, after one night of sleeping badly on the new bed, Les had had enough saying that it was too hard and therefore I was asked if I would consider changing beds as the new bed would be firmer and so much better for me. On our visit to buy the beds, we did look at cookers because I was still managing on the dreadful two-burner stove and the temperamental oven, but Les still did not succumb. I wondered what would Derek say when he arrived, apparently I was the talk of many of their French dinner parties as to how I managed to produce, a meal under near stone age conditions.

Dave made us all laugh telling us the story of how on a previous visit to France he had bought a tin of l'escargots, which he gave to a friend and on his return to England the friend promptly forgot them and left them in the car. The tin was damaged and the snails began to leak out on the car floor producing an awful smell.

At first they were unable to find the cause of the smell because the tin was wedged under one of the seats.

Eventually they found the problem and removed it, but the owner of the car, was not amused because he had to replace his carpet to get rid of the smell.

Fran and Dee were due to arrive on the Monday morning, so I prepared lunch of soup, ham, salad, paté, cheese and of course the baguette, knowing this to be their customary lunch. I knew we would be drinking wine with a meal when our friend Dee was present. When we are on our own, we only have wine in the evening because drinking at lunchtime always makes us sleepy. However, Dee always says if you drink rosé it won't affect you because it is only light - if you believe that you will believe anything. However, this theory is subject to the quantity consumed and he is renowned for his long after lunch naps. Lunchtime came and went without the arrival of Fran or Dee. I was worried that they might have met with an accident and unfortunately we did not possess a telephone at that time. It was decided we would buy a mobile when we returned home. When the guests eventually arrived, they said they had been waiting for something of importance in the post and unfortunately they had trouble with their car. Dave had a look at their car on the next day and found that one of the front bearings was worn but Dave did say he thought it would be good for another 1000 miles. This would enable them to get home to the UK at the end of the month where the car was having its MOT. Fran had arrived as usual laden with food including a joint of cold lamb, cheese, sweets (she is very good on the old puddings) and I could see Dave's mouth watering in anticipation. I had prepared the evening meal early on, and when I had been shopping in the morning I had bought what I had thought was self raising flour but the pastry I made with it for the apple pie, was a disaster. It was like eating leather, apparently it was plain flour used for bread making and when looking for self-raising flour, it must have `levant' on the packet - I was learning. Luckily we had the sweets which Fran had brought - so all was not lost.

That evening we talked over old times with ample vin rouge flowing to stimulate the memories of the incidents when they first took on the renovation of their house in Deux Sevres. One such incident, was of the cooker extraction hood which required at least six successive attempts to assemble and install. This was after a lunch with an ample supply of wine and four people's different interpretations of the instructions. Well, as the imaginations began to blur true facts, we thought it was time to retire to bed about midnight.

Because the bedroom walls had plasterboard only on one side, no sound insulation could be fitted until the other plasterboard skin had been fixed. As we lay in bed you could hear every sound and I mean every sound from the other rooms. These sounds included snoring from Les - there was only one answer - you had just got to get to sleep before the others. We knew Dave's broken ribs, damaged before the visit, were still hurting him because when he rolled over in his sleep, he used to let out a yell. The first night Fran and Dee stayed and I asked Fran if she had slept well. Her response was " O.K until I heard the dawn patrol" " what do you mean" I asked". She replied " haven't you noticed when one of the men gets up, for the toilet, the other two follow suit, unlike the women who tip toe quietly so as not to disturb anyone, the chaps troop just like a herd of elephants as in the jungle book `dawn patrol'. I said that I would listen particularly for this event and I found that she was right.

We have a visit every day from the small farm dog, Belle and on one particular morning, I had left some rubbish out in a bag which I intended taking to the communal dustbin, located at the end of the road, but I had been busy and forgotten about it. I then heard a shout from Les saying that Belle had gone off with a whole chicken carcass from the rubbish bag. We had eaten chicken the previous day. I was very worried since back home, we never gave chicken bones to dogs because I understood they could splinter which appears to be a fallacy. "Quickly, help me catch her and take the chicken off her" I said to Les. "No way" said Les "she will not let you take it from her" I followed her as best I could calling for her to come to me offering her a biscuit but she wagged her tail but would not part with her chicken. I watched her constantly that day but she did not appear to have come to any harm and I remained worried for the week but she was fine. I don't think it had anything to do with the chicken, but every night about the same time, just after we had all retired to bed, Belle would start to howl and this would go on for what seemed like ages. I asked René, what was upsetting her. He replied " la lune" (the moon) "when the moon is full she always does it".

I was in the kitchen one morning and I spotted something on the floor, it was a dead mouse. David had been putting pellets down to kill off any vermin that might come inside the house. Dave soon got rid of the remains of our little guest but it left me a little on edge for the rest of the week, imagining mice in every nook and cranny.

On the Wednesday, we all went to Rennes for the day with the purpose of purchasing windows for the new bedrooms to install on the next visit when we would have the time to make holes in the 2 feet thick walls. We had received planning permission for the windows without any queries. I must admit Les had done some very thorough drawings and photographs when he was seeking permission and it had obviously paid off.

In Rennes, we were looking for a large super store called Le Roi Merlin, which our French electrician had told us about. He had given us some directions but unfortunately Rennes was extremely busy and Les is not the best at taking instructions from back seat drivers and don't forget this was France with different road markings to ours. I think he forgot on several occasions and Dee, who had been driving in France for many years, was getting agitated. "Les, you are driving in the bus lane - you are not meant to drive in this lane". Well to cut the story short, Les changed lanes without looking and we nearly got a car go into us broadside on. " Oh God" said I " what has God got to do with it" said Les " we will soon find out Les, if you carry on like this" I said. We found Le Roi Merlin which sold almost everything and we began the search for windows. We could not find exactly the sizes we needed but I did find some nice colourful tiles for the shower room, which was a consolation. Derek was busy looking at circular stairways. When we left the store we stopped at a little Bistro for lunch and we had baguettes and a drink and after we had finished Les said to me " you can drive".

We set off and it is customary on our trips for Dave to navigate because he does do it well but on this occasion I had at least two people giving me the directions so consequently I went off at the wrong turn on the motorway. Eventually I got on the correct road and arrived home with plenty of stress but no further trouble.

That evening we paid a visit to Mimi's bar and Derek enjoyed himself and gave the bar his seal of approval. During the course of the evening we were introduced to an Englishman sitting at the bar. My first impression of the man was that he had finished work and spent the rest of the day in the bar. He was tall and broad, with dark hair and blue eyes and had obviously had a lot to drink however, my party was quite merry with the exception of myself - the driver!. He came over to join us, Les bought a round of drinks and asked the stranger what he would like to drink. The drinks duly arrived and I asked him where he came from. He said he was from Cornwall and we asked what he was doing here. He told us he had bought 3 cottages just up the road for only 180000 francs. I thought that these were cheap although he said that they were in need of doing up. He had just finished putting a state of the art kitchen in, obviously more up market than ours, with the units we had acquired from our friends Betty and Mike that they were otherwise sending to the tip. Les can't resist a bargain - say no more.

As the evening progressed, our new friend became more talkative and we learnt that he had a partner of 12 years standing who had a son but recently her son had died tragically. He did not say what happened to his partner who was now back in the U.K. and he said he would never return to England. He did tell us that an Englishwoman who was a rich widow, living in a local chateau, had befriended him. He asked us if we had any wood we could spare him Les said he was sure he could find him some. The next day he came to the house at 9am when we were hardly up and I made a quick escape leaving him to Les. As it so happened I could not offer him a drink we were out of coffee that made it seem to be a cool reception but he did get some wood. He was a different person when sober and the visit was soon over. He departed with his wood and we have not seen him again.

      Fran had kindly offered to make my curtains for the French house. I was very pleased because sewing was not my strong point and Dee agreed to do all the measuring and put up the wooden curtain poles. Fran and I cut out the material for the curtains to go in the lounge which were pretty shades of pale blue, mauve and primrose, to complement the primrose coloured walls. When they were finished and hung they looked attractive and at last the place was beginning to look like a home.

That evening Fran, Dave and me played scrabble and Les had gone to pay the roofer and was away for the whole evening. Normally paying a bill to a contractor does not take as long but the thought of playing scrabble may have had something to do with it. Dee was busy reading, so as the three of us got ready to play. Dave said " I haven't played for ages" He was having us on and every game he wiped the floor with us - these Scots are a bit canny and some of the words he used had a flavour of Gaelic not to be found in an Oxford dictionary.

Fran and Dee went home the next morning after David had changed the tyres to put the better ones on the front of their vehicle. After they had departed I decided to put the topcoat on the paint work in the lounge. At first I was going to paint it white, but Dave had remarked he thought it would be too pale so I decided on blue to tone with my curtains. I purchased the paint at the local DIY store. The paint was water based and went on easily. When finished I thought it looked a very professional job.

Our visit was coming to a close and we all admitted we just did not want to return home. The evening before we were due to depart, Les invited René for a drink and to impress him with the work we had done. We had an entertaining evening including finding out that René, was something of a comedian. We were all beginning to contribute in French and to understand each other's sense of humour. By the end of the evening we were all roaring with laughter. David tried to explain to René, that he was going to build a fire basket for the fire place but René, could not understand, so David disappeared and came back with a drawing of the fireplace on a piece of plaster board. René, said, " please sign it" and we all laughed since prior to this remark, we had shown René, some signed sketches that Robert had drawn of the Josselin chateau and the lake by our house. We explained that Robert was an artist as well as a builder and since he had signed all of his pictures René, was teasing Dave into signing his plasterboard drawing. The conversation then got on to the size of Les's girth and René, proceeded to show off his biceps, and Les said " oh pop eye" Dave taps René on the shoulder pointing to my legs and said " Olive" to shrieks of laughter.

We were away the next morning by 9am deciding to visit Mont St Michel, on the way to the ferry arriving at midday. It was fascinating and well worth the visit. Mont-St-Michel Abbey /

fortress and village is a remarkable feature, clinging to a needle of granite presenting an image of breathtaking beauty. A causeway reaches it and on this particular day, it was scattered with spring flowers. Dave and myself purchased paintings of the rock with the church at the top. We only paid a few francs for them. My intention was to frame the print and place it on the lounge wall alongside the drawing of the Chateau at Josselin, which Robert had drawn for me. We have several prints of various Chateaux we have visited including the chateau at Saumur and the print of the aerial view of Carcassonne and a print of the Chateau at Chenonceau. When we visit a place of interest, we try to buy a print as a momento. After leaving Mont St Michel we drove on to Cherbourg to catch the boat to England. On the boat Les recognised a gentleman he had worked with many years ago but remembered that he was a bit of a bore and the thought of 6 hours in his company would be too long and thus avoided contact until just before we docked. However it was useful to catch up with the news of the other people who used to work for their Company. In addition he told us a strange story. He had been at a dinner party with friends and one of them had been talking about a trip over to France. This person had a conversation with someone on the boat who told him about a man, his wife, two children and grannie who were going on holiday to France with their caravan. As they neared the ferry port the man asked his wife to collect up all the passports and much to their dismay, grannie had not brought hers along. This is the dreaded oversight for all would-be ferry passengers.

Not wanting to miss his holiday, the son suggested that they should hide grannie in the caravan where she would also be comfortable for the crossing and this would avoid passport problems at the French port. Reluctantly this solution was accepted. After arriving in France, they drove on until they found a suitable parking area. The son opened up the caravan to let grannie join them in the car.

Unfortunately grannie had died during the crossing! This caused panic to set in amongst the rest of the family and was followed by a decision to come clean and report the circumstances to the French police. They uncoupled the caravan in a car park near the next town and drove off to find a police station where they made a statement of all the facts. The police escorted them back to the car park where they had left the caravan only to find that it had been stolen.

Les's friend was waiting to meet with the storyteller to hear the outcome of this debacle. We came to a unanimous decision that Les's friend was not such a bore after all. Perhaps he was just a good storyteller.

We were planning to return to France on 21 April 1999, and this time we would be sailing over night from Portsmouth to St Malo, leaving Portsmouth in the evening at 8.30 pm. On this trip we would be taking David and Ray with us, since we were anxious to get as much work done as possible this time, because Les was due to go into hospital for a hip replacement. Because of the uncertain results of this, we were not sure when we would be going back to France. Our objective this time was to finish tiling the kitchen floor and to cover the wall surfaces which at the moment, was just rough stone work. We were considering sticking plaster board to them and papering them. The local French builders said that when you put the plasterboard up you fill the joins with a product called Enduit, which there does not seem to be a UK equivalent. It appears to be a filler/adhesive, which makes the walls smooth enough to paper or emulsion. David would be concentrating on tiling of the kitchen floor, whilst Les and Ray fixed the plaster board down stairs and chipped out the walls upstairs for Dave to put in the new windows. My job this time would be to decorate the bathroom. We had arranged to leave Worcester about 4.30pm and we would stop on the way for fish and chips since this time we have got Ray with us and he likes his chips, but I am changing his eating habits slowly.

Prior to our departure Les and I went for a drive one weekend and we happened to pass a yard full of old wood and various products from demolition. Les wanted to buy some hard wood to use as lintels above the three new windows we had planned to put in next trip. We picked four pieces of oak and asked the old boy Cecil if he would cut them to the required lengths and this he did at a cost of £2 each. We were taking Dave's arc welder this time to repair the cement mixer. We needed this for mixing mortar for fitting the windows. Les had arranged to meet Dave at the local pub the night before departure, to discuss what tools would be needed on this trip as space in the car was limited. There was much discussion with friends in the pub on how the window apertures should be made. Unlike over here, the walls are 2 ft thick with stone on the outer surfaces and rubble in the middle and we would require props to support the wall above them. They decided in the end that it would not be necessary to use acrow props. By now we were getting into the swing of things in relation to our trips to France and knowing what items of food to take over and what to buy over there. For example, I now buy my self raising flour here after my disaster with the pastry made with French flour.

The films from the last trip were developed and we had some very good snaps showing the progress we have made on the house. We were given some helpful advice from Frederick, our French electrician, on where to buy windows cheaper than at Rennes. Les and I had been busy working out the French for asking Yvonne, our neighbour, to ask her gardener if he will cut our grass for us on a regular basis. I hope we get the French correct or we may have the cows back to do it.

CHAPTER EIGHT

Stuck in the Mud

Our next trip was in May 1999, a month later than planned due to my husband's work commitments in the UK. When we left Kempsey the rain was bucketing down. It had taken the two lads some time, in the rain, to secure the two sets of chest of draws on to the roof rack of the car. With the weather so bad they had to make sure the plastic covers went over securely because one of the chests was full of our bedding, which we needed to be kept dry. We stopped, as usual, for a coffee just outside of Newbury, continuing on our journey reaching Portsmouth in time to buy a take-away fish and chips supper before we joined the ferry. Unfortunately we were asked to embark on the boat straight away allowing no time to eat our chips before we were on the car deck. We were hastily eating them when the boat was due to leave port after which no one is allowed to remain on the car deck. It was quite amusing because one of the French stewardesses saw us frantically eating our chips and tapped the car window and said "give us a chip I haven't had a good chip for ages". We went up in the lift to find our couchettes, which were certainly an improvement on the last trip, with the back rest lifting back and a foot rest which was adjustable. We piled our hand luggage in the seats and went off to find the bar. The cabarets in the bars at night were usually entertaining and this night there was a singer who had a powerful voice and an illusionist who to quote the boys was assisted by " a cracker" although somewhat over weight for disappearing into the illusionists little box. Both acts were quite enjoyable. In the corner of the bar the TV was on, showing a football match between Manchester United and Juventus and Manchester United won 3.2 - thank the lord.

When I left the car deck on the ferry, I had put on my seasickness bracelets that I had worn on the previous trip and where they had worked wonders, but on that occasion, the sea had been calm. This night it was a different story, since after leaving Portsmouth about two hours, and at the apparent point where the currents in the Channel converge, I could feel the boat begin to pitch and roll. I looked at Ray who was a paler shade than usual and I was feeling queasy. I expressed my concern and thought it best if I retired and Ray was in agreement.

The sturdy Scot said "what's the matter we ye girl - its as calm as a mill pond". Les said " you are wearing your anti seasickness bands they should be good they cost £7.50" Les and Dave remained at the bar while Ray and I went up to the couchettes where Ray managed to sleep, but not me. I could feel those fish and chips sitting like a lump of lead in my chest. Eventually I went to the cloakroom where, luckily for me, there was no one else about - what a waste of good fish and chips.

I made myself go back to the couchettes and tried to sleep - without much hope of succeeding - I decided to take a sea legs tablet and I slept for an hour, waking as Les and Dave returned.

I went to the ladies room, took another sea leg and for the rest of the journey I was O.K.- so much for the wrist bands.

At 6am, we where back in calm waters and we all ate breakfast, disembarking at 7am and we made only one stop for coffee. I drove half way, but was glad when Les took over since the tablets had made me tired and we arrived at Quelneuc mid morning - early for once. As we drove along the lane leading to our house, René, saw our car from a distant field where he was driving his tractor.

He welcomed us by a blast from his horn and a wave. We were not surprised that he could recognise us knowing from experience that we were likely to be the only car with two dressing tables on the roof rack.

We unpacked the car and the lads set to work whilst I prepared lunch and made up the beds. The floors had accumulated the usual amount of dust for our arrival. After lunch, Les and Ray went to purchase some more plasterboard and Dave commenced laying the floor tiles in the kitchen and I went out to our local super market to stock up with food. That evening we did not go out but sat chatting by the fire. Dave and I tried a half-hearted attempt at the Times crossword. Needless to say we did not complete pretending it was not so much our lack of knowledge but more to our lack of sleep from the night before which was catching up on us. I was the first to retire and I went out like a light and the next thing I recall, was Les asking if I wanted a cup of tea. I said I did and asked what the time was. It was 8am, which of course is only 7am at home. David was up as usual and bright as a cricket whilst Ray, like me, was still three parts asleep. Les is always active when he gets over to France and becomes a different person, so I thought I best get up and show willing by getting the breakfasts.

After eating I went with Les to find the shop were we could purchase the windows from the advice given to us by our French electrician.

The journey to Mèdrineac was straightforward and the countryside we passed through was beautiful and we had travelled some 20 miles having met only three vehicles on the road. Where in England would this be the case?

At the store we looked for the windows but unfortunately the only ones they had were not a suitable size. However, our journey was not wasted because we purchased a foldaway bed for £29 and I spotted some very nice rugs at a reasonable price, which would be ideal for in front of the old fireplace. We returned home and I prepared lunch and it was decided that in the afternoon, Les would go to Vannes on his own to look for windows and I would start to paint the bathroom. The bathroom was large and it would take me some time, unlike at home where, I could splash the emulsion on right away, these walls required filling and sanding in various places, if the job was to look right.

In Vannes Les could not find the place which had been recommended to him, so he decided to travel to Rennes which was about the same distance to the east of Quelneuc as Vannes was to the west. I prepared the evening meal for 7pm but Les did not return until 8.15pm. We were all getting worried by this time, thinking he may have got lost. However, it transpired the traffic had been very heavy coming out of Rennes and `Voila'- he had two windows but they did not have the third one, which we needed, in the size required. We could install these two and get another window later. David and Ray in the meantime were making a good job of plaster boarding and filling the gaps in the kitchen plasterboard in readiness for the plasterer - if we ever find one in France.

The kitchen floor-tiling job was made difficult with the kitchen in constant use. Dave was trying to be helpful by only tiling in certain areas so that I had access to the kitchen sink and of course the cooker. However, each day the cooker was in a different place, due to the parts of the walls to which plaster board was being erected. Consequently, I stepped back on one of the new tiles, which had not set yet, and it cracked. Dave was OK about it but when I repeated the exercise a day later, he must have thought "stupid woman".

I was disappointed with the colour of the emulsion I had brought over from England since it was supposed to be apricot but it looked pink when it was on the bathroom walls. Still it would make a good undercoat, albeit expensive and I would need to be more careful with my checking of emulsion colours in the future.

In the evening we went up to Mimi's bar and I tried a local drink of Almagneac, Les chose Calvados, Dave tried the Ricard and Ray as always, adhered to his Coke.

We chatted with the locals with many of them recognising us from our previous visits. They were interested in the progress we were making on the houses by the lake. I think that they were still a little puzzled as to why we wanted to renovate such ruins when there were new houses for sale nearby.

Mimi had refurbished and rearranged the bar in our absence. A local art teacher had painted some murals for her depicting French men in 1950's caps and jackets sitting outside bars and some other street scenes. This added character to the bar and provided a topic for conversation.

We told her that we were very impressed and more of this should be done in English pubs. Perhaps a cricket scene may be more appropriate in England.

Next morning we were up early and there were no hangovers so we must be getting back in tune with the French way of life. The day was sunny and we sat out in the garden after lunch. Work was progressing well and I had completed painting the bathroom. The kitchen floor tiles were nearly all laid. The floor in the kitchen had been a real problem due to it not being level because the concrete surface had not been skimmed after it was laid claimed David. He levelled the surface with the tile adhesive, which had to be very thick in parts making it costly at £20 per bag. Les and Ray continued on the never-ending erection of plaster boarding. By now they were becoming experts, finding it easier to place the bottom plasterboard sheet in first. They then put the MAP adhesive on the wall above this for the next sheet to be lifted into place.

We had been given a tip by René that when plaster boarding the north facing walls, put extra MAP on the back of the plaster boards to allow for more circulation of air. The success of this however could only be measured over a long period of time.

On this visit, I had brought my own flour from England, so I decided to make an apple pie, but I had forgotten to bring a rolling pin and I resorted to using an empty wine bottle. It is really amazing that you think you have remembered to buy everything, which you use at home, but on each trip there is always something forgotten. I expect we shall become fully equipped in the kitchen by the time the house is fully renovated.

I was beginning to feel tired since I was not used to so much manual work but I was not the only one of our team because the men were feeling the same. I decided to take time off for a walk by the lake. It is amazing what a change of scenery will do to relieve tiredness. When I reached the lake, there were two fishing boats moored but no sign of anyone. It is always so quiet and peaceful there. The only other sign of life was a large heron waiting to catch his evening meal, poised at the water edge, statue like reminding one of a little stooping old man. It is a surprisingly large bird with a very wide wing span displayed as I approached. The countryside around our hamlet is varied and very beautiful with rich rolling pastures, large areas of forest and many lakes and rivers being a land of farmers living in small compact Breton hamlets.

The houses are mainly of granite or limestone, sometimes rendered having tall-pitched roofs of slate or tiles to enable them to withstand the buffeting of the Atlantic winds. I remember Yvonne telling me to close the barn door before we left for England. Mistakenly I had thought she wanted the door closed because of thieves, but it was the vent I discovered later was the wind which will blow a roof off quite easily if it gets inside outbuildings.

After our evening meal that day, we decided to see if we could find the road that went around the lake and we made several unsuccessful attempts but eventually we did come across a road which looked promising. I was driving at the time and as we neared the lake I thought the ground looked soggy. I said to Les " I think we should turn back". He said, "no, just go on a little to where you can turn - over there." As we continued, the road became very wet and Les like me began to wonder if we were doing the right thing. He said "just keep going - what ever you do don't stop". I kept going as instructed and the wheels began to spin without the car moving. Dave said "shall I take over" and I readily agreed. Ray and I got out of the car and attempted to push while Dave did some fast manoeuvres and eventually he got the car out. By this time Ray and I and the car were splattered with mud. "How embarrassing" said Ray " getting stuck in the mud, I wish I had brought the camera." All I was worried about was the state of the car, which I would need to clean, before I had to explain to anyone, what had happened. We made our way carefully picking out the drier parts of the track, back to the main road. We all agreed that we could do with a drink to help us recover from our mishap. I suggested the Irish pub in Ploërmel. When we arrived, there was confusion over the entrance since the doors appeared to be locked. One of these had a bell with a notice above. When we rang the bell nothing happened but eventually we realised that it was up to the would-be customers to push the door open. There were no customers in the bar prompting Les to ask if we could get in the bar next door, thinking there would be another room with customers in it. The barman looked puzzled, saying " non" and wondering why we had come in for a drink if we were asking to go next door. Les makes it worse by asking what is upstairs, meaning is their a restaurant or some entertainment. The barman said they had a room. " What sort of a room" said Les. " a room " repeated the barman. Well, I started to giggle told Les to shut up and said under my breath, for him to leave it and order the drinks. This is the problem when you are not able to converse sufficiently in another language, you can very easily be misunderstood. Thankfully Les took the hint and ordered the drinks. Considering that it was called the Irish pub, I asked the barman if he had been to Ireland, trying to make conversation." non" he said which ended that conversation. We sat down at one of the wooden beer barrels being used as tables with our drinks and after a few minutes much to our amazement the barman joined us and began speaking in very good English. It transpired that he had been in the pub for about three months, prior to this he had been in Milan were he had been studying financial management" I am an Accountant" said Les " my course was nothing so grand as that" he retorted. After Milan he had been in Nice for a time and we found the stories of his experiences most interesting and when we said our farewells we promised to return.

On the way home Dave drove the car and to my delight he said "I see Jill what you mean about this car being under powered" " I am glad someone agrees with me - there you are Les, I told you so" I said continuing on with " I am definitely changing it at the end of the year" This comment leads into another saga for my next book.

It was only nine o'clock so we decided to call to see Mimi since we pass her bar on the way home for a night cap but the bar was unusually busy and noisy with some good natured but boisterous French youngsters. We did not remain there long returning home for a cup of coffee whilst we discussed the projects for the following day. One of these was to knock a piece of the wall out and put in the first new window but we had not anticipated the rain would be so heavy. Because the weather was bad we all continued working on the kitchen and I was busy putting crepi on the wall inside the front door. Crepi is the French version of Artex but I did not solve the problem of applying it evenly I think more went on the floor than on the wall. Unfortunately, I did make the mistake of letting Dave see me trying to lever the lid off the paint tin with what I thought was Les's chisel. I said to Dave with my finger to my lips "don't breath a word to Les" "good god woman, that is not

Les's chisel - that is mine and I have just spent half an hour sharpening it" said Dave. I exclaimed "Oh merde" and quickly resorted to an old kitchen knife.

After lunch I began preparations since we were expecting friends Fran and Derek again the following day. We always looked forward to their visits as they were very helpful and there is always a lot of lighthearted banter between everyone. Dave had christened Dee the clerk of works and of course it has stuck with his habit of coming up quietly and watching closely what the workmen were doing. I am sure he does it on purpose. Fran and Dee arrived laden with food as usual including cake, wine, meat pie and cheese. We had our evening meal early which consisted of beef done in Calvados on the hob slowly, with onions and carrots and a few mushrooms and cooked this way, meat is always tender. We had roast and new potatoes and the usual vegetables of peas and cauliflower and for sweet, I had made a fruit jelly with creme frêche - the French answer to cream. I heated some of Fran's mince pies and we followed these with good old English cheddar, which is still unobtainable in the local shops in our part of France. When the meal was finished, our visitors were anxious to see the Irish pub for themselves after hearing of our experiences there. On this evening, there were more people in the bar and the atmosphere was buzzing with our friendly barman welcoming us with handshakes all round, as is the French custom. When we had ordered drinks, he asked Les if we had any children who collected beer mats. He replied that one of the grand children did and consequently he was given a large quantity of different and unusual beer mats to take home after the local customers had examined these.

The following day the rain had stopped so we decided to start work on knocking out the hole in the wall for the first window. This was far from straight forward unlike putting in windows at home. The walls here are very old and thick and the clay type mortar makes the removal of stones a little precarious. Dave marked out where the window was to go, making sure it was not under any of the main beams, which were carrying the weight of the roof. The French aluminium ladder we had bought had square section rungs and when it is leaning at an angle against the wall, the edges of the treads come in the middle of one's feet. By the end of the day, Dave was complaining of sore feet through standing on the edge of the square rungs. The window was marked out to Les's satisfaction. David measured 10 inches down from the original wall plate on which the rafters were bearing, He then carefully began taking out the stones on the outer skin of the wall. When there was a sufficient gap to take the depth of the oak lintel. He measured 48 inches long by 4 inches square section. The lintel had to be carefully lifted into place whilst the stones above were supported with pieces of 1" square section wood placed vertically.

These pieces of wood were knocked inside the wall by the lintel being pushed into the space, which they had been supporting. The mortar securing the stones was only clay, lime and sand (the house being over 200 years old) made it more unstable than brick bonded walls- especially when someone who will be nameless was excavating the internal wall like a demolition expert. After holes had been made, the bedrooms were a little chilly at night - being open to the elements. Making these window apertures was more difficult than one would expect. The inside lintels were pre-stressed concrete blocks from the local French builder's merchant.

However, all went well with only a few tense moments and it took us 4 days to get the windows in and on the fourth day it rained and they did not leak anywhere, much to our relief. I must admit the new windows transformed the look of the house and all we needed now was a new front door but we are making do with a lick of paint on the old one for the moment.

New windows overlooking fields

Cows looking at new windows

Ray at this time was busy spreading red shale on the driveways around the three properties. We had obtained the shale from René, who had kindly tipped it from his trailer at various points around the houses so we did not need to carry barrow loads everywhere. When the shale had been raked and flattened it served the purpose by preventing a lot of mud getting into the house. Derek had been busy strimming the grass for us which would have been a big help if his strimmer had not packed up. Ray used one of the antique sickles we found in the out building to cut the grass and scrub since it was much too long to attempt a lawnmower on it.

That evening Les seemed quiet as if he had something on his mind. It transpired that René, had asked him if he could buy our land. His cows were already on it and I was not very eager to sell, but after talking it through we decided to sell some of it but retain enough for reasonable size gardens. It was agreed to meet with the estate agent from which we had bought the properties, because of his knowledge of prices for and his ability to speak English on a future visit to France. Les went to pay for the shale but René, would not take the money. This was awkward when his family had been so helpful and we did not want to offend them.

The days passed quickly and it was time for Fran and Dee to go but we would be seeing them again soon in England at their youngest daughter's wedding. When they had gone, I felt more able to help clear up after the installation of the windows. The dust from the windows, which was mainly rubble from the interiors of the walls and plasterboard cutting dust, had been horrendous. The lads had removed the worst but there was still a lot to clear away. The dust got everywhere but one consolation was that this was the last major job on this house and the rest of the work we hoped would be relatively clean but this eventually turned out to be too optimistic.

On the Friday, we decided to invite René, and Yvonne, for a drink and a bite to eat in the evening. We also invited Hélén and

Alfred the couple living across the road from us. Hélén is a typical French lady- dark haired and petite, possibly in her late sixties who we usually meet each day riding her bicycle frantically through the hamlet, dressed in black - reminding me of a blackbird in flight. Her husband Alfred has grey, straight hair, heavily built and is a retired bricklayer and a man of few words. In the morning, we had been to Hélén's house for a glass of wine and biscuits. It does concentrate the mind on speaking French, since they do not speak any English but it is in these types of situations where we learn most of our French. Hélén and her husband are deaf, so this only adds to our language difficulties, but we all joined in the conversation although with a good measure of guess-work and nodding hopefully at the appropriate points. The evening seemed to be enjoyed by all, but Ray was quiet. He said to me later that when he got home, he was going to learn French.

On Saturday we finished working and we tidied up by 2pm, so we decided to go to La Baule. An administrative re-organisation 25 years ago separated part of the south of Brittany from the rest. The result of this was that La Baule then belonged to the neighbouring region of Pays de la Loire. In doing so, it had taken away one of Brittany's biggest and most fashionable seaside resorts. The vast stretch of sand at La Baule goes on for miles, giving beach lovers plenty of choice. We went on the beach and Les had a paddle while we all watched him. There were people in swimming making us all wish we had bought our swimming costumes and later we had a drink at the beach side restaurant. It was lovely sitting in the sun watching the sea and the world go by. We left La Baule and went to visit Guerande which Les and I had visited before. However Dave and Ray appreciated the town completely encircled by the 15th century ramparts with four gateways providing access to the old streets containing many charming houses and shops. This is a very quaint town with lots to see with little shops, which intrigue me since they are so different from back at home. I bought us all large ice creams, which we enjoyed whilst watching a line of little children, dressed in white entering the very old church to take their first Holy Communion. We returned home via Roquefort- en- Terre, famed for its picturesque streets and lovely squares of 16th and 17th century houses, wreathed in flowers throughout the summer. It has been many times winner of best-kept village in the Brittany competition. However when we arrived here the lads were fast asleep in the back of the car, I just hadn't the heart to awaken them, since they were so tired. We arrived home ready for our evening meal. Fortunately, I had put the meat in the slow cooker, so all I had to do was cook the vegetables.

I had promised to do pancakes for them on this night, so Dave volunteered to whisk the batter. After we had eaten, we retired early, ready for our early start in the morning to return home.

The following morning the weather was fine and we left about 7am, waved off by all our neighbours with Hélén still in her night-dress and rollers." Bon Voyage" they shouted and we said, "where in England would you receive this treatment".

The journey to the boat was fairly uneventful and the sea was relatively like a millpond - thank goodness. When we passed the Isle of Wight, I gave a little mental wave, remembering all the years I had spent there with memories both happy and sad, flooding back. Once back home we were making plans for our next visit to France and by the way, we were trying to decide on a name for the next house with many contributions from David.

CHAPTER NINE

Water in the Diesel

Our next booking to France was 21 June 1999 with a middle of the night departure from Kempsey, to arrive at Portsmouth for 6.30am in time to catch the Catamaran for Cherbourg departing at 7am and a crossing time of only 2 hours 45 minutes. I was taking my friend Joan with us who agreed to help me with the decorating and hopefully the cooking. Joan has been a friend of mine for 20 years and I first met her when I went to work at the same hospital. She was in charge of night nursing staff and I was responsible for day nursing staff - we hit it off straight away. It is a family joke that Joan resembles Ann Robinson (following her quotations of "you are the weakest link - goodbye"). David joined us to finish the last of the plaster boarding and kitchen floor tiling.

I understood from friends over in France that currently the weather was very warm and sunny which would suit us, as we always look forward to France where the sun is warm enough to eat our meals outside under the old bay tree. David had promised us a barbecue done army style and we hoped to keep him to it.

On the day before leaving, Joan came to stay the night with us so that we could go to bed around 9pm to give us 6 hours rest. Les went as usual to our local supermarket to get enough diesel to travel only to Portsmouth because it was more than a third cheaper to fill up after we had landed in France. I had been to my music in the afternoon and used the car, noticing that the gauge was registering almost empty. After Les put the diesel in the tank, we finished loading up the car and roof rack with our usual array of furniture and luggage before he went to meet David at a little country pub called the Huntsman which was just across the common. The reason for this was, he claimed, to make sure that

David would be ready to leave at 3am with his passport (we never let him forget the missing passport incident on his first trip). Joan and I went to bed and we were just dozing off when I heard vehicles and voices at the end of the drive. I looked out from the bedroom window and much to my amazement there was Dave with his pickup towing my car so I quickly went downstairs to find out what the problem was. Les said that the car had cut out when he was going over the common. Luckily a woman came by in her car, asked what the problem was and he explained that he couldn't move the car. She said that she couldn't give him a lift back to the pub because she had her two dogs in the car but she offered to go to the pub to give a message to Dave that Les needed help with his car on the common. The lady called out in the pub for someone called David to go to his friend who had broken down with a load of furniture on the roof rack, on the common. Dave made his way to where the car was stranded. After checking the car engine and concluding that nothing could be done in the dark, on the common, they towed the car back to our house. Les came in the house to telephone Green Flag vehicle recovery that arrived about 1am, checked the car engine and the man said he thought it was the fuel pump. He was unable to do anything to the car that night since it would be necessary to have the repair done at a garage and that he would return at 8 am to tow the car to a specialist diesel engine garage in Malvern. We unpacked the furniture on the roof rack, hoping we would not have to unpack the car boot. We were all upset at the prospect of missing the boat and the next morning Les rang P&O Ferries to explain why this had happened and to change the booking to the same time on the following morning. In the meantime the car problem was being checked by Malvern garage and we arranged to ring them at 12 midday to confirm that the car would be ready, in time to catch the next ferry. However, the garage rang us at 10am, to tell us that we would not be going to France for three days since the pump had been badly damaged by excessive amounts of water in the fuel. The tank had to be removed and emptied. When this had been done, the garage said that 90% of the contents was water. The water had gone through the fuel filter damaging the engine and the bill would be £1,300. Les had kept his receipt for the diesel and we went to see the manager of the supermarket where he had purchased the diesel but he was not available. We spoke with a duty manager who filled in a complaint form and we were told they would be in contact with us.

The next day we went to the garage to check the progress on the car repairs and were dismayed to see all the items of our luggage scattered over the greasy garage floor.

Apparently the petrol tank could only be removed from inside the car boot. We thought it advisable to collect up our luggage from the garage floor and take it home in my husband's car. Fortunately my car was repaired a little earlier than they originally thought and we collected it the next morning. We then felt confident enough to fix another ferry booking by telephone.

When we set off to France eventually, we were unable to go on the catamaran since it was fully booked and we were all most disappointed in missing what would have been a new experience in ferry crossing. We sailed on the Pride of Hampshire ferry to Cherbourg overnight with no cabins available and so we were in reclining seats which are hopeless when you want to sleep. Making things worse, we were situated at the top of the boat and there was just a thin door between us and the deck and all night we were cold. The men slept better than Joan and me but then they always do - I suspect it is the alcohol content in their blood which they consume the night before. We went down to breakfast at 6am but we didn't feel like a full English breakfast so we settled for cornflakes and croissants. The coffee was foul, (luke warm and thick). Things could only get better. We arrived at Cherbourg on time in brilliant sunshine and blue sky at 7am and the temperature already beginning to rise. We broke our journey for coffee and by this time the sun was really hot, making us think that at last summer had begun. We arrived at Quelneuc at 12.30pm and got out of the car and started to unpack straight away. When we got inside the house, Joan's face was a picture and although I had warned her of what to expect, I don't think she believed me. However, four hours later, with a meal inside her and a good gin and tonic, things looked different, especially after some thorough cleaning and she breathed a sigh of relief and said that it now looked like home and how I imagined it would be.

When I walked down the lane to show Joan the lake, she was very surprised at its nearness to the house, its vastness and its beauty. During our first morning in Quelneuc, we had several French visitors, which is customary when we arrive, since they want to know how we are and just as eagerly find out whom we have brought with us on this occasion. Joan was surprised how well we were able to communicate with them and also how much she could understand of the conversation - thanks a little to our French lessons. That evening, Joan prepared the freshly picked strawberries, which we had purchased from a small cottage on the way from the ferry. This involved lacing the strawberries with her homemade elderflower wine, which made a super sweet. For the main course, we had my homemade steak pie, with cauliflower, carrots and mashed potatoes, with the very good local supermarket vin rouge. Because the weather was so good, we ate all our meals, outside under the bay tree on that day. We agreed that it was good to be back!

That evening we promised to take Joan to see the chateau in the typically French town of Josselin. However, we were delayed a little because Dave was part way through putting down the self-levelling compound on the kitchen floor in readiness for laying the tiles on the next day. Also Les was organising the workroom, in order to enable tools to be found more easily for the work to be done in the days ahead.

When we eventually arrived in Josselin, we went into the old square and sat outside at one of the many tables lining the pavements and ordered our drinks. The air was so warm and still but by now we were all tired and all we wanted to do was go to bed, but first we wished to show Joan the Chateau. Fortunately she had the benefit of seeing it bathed in moonlight and was duly impressed.

We returned home by 11.30pm and I made hot drinks for everyone and after we finished these, we all retired to our beds. We slept soundly, to be awakened by Dave at 7.30am with our early morning cup of tea, which he made after already having walked to the lake and looking as fresh as a daisy. I got up soon after and prepared breakfast which we ate outside as the sun was up and warming the early morning. After breakfast Les went to order sand and gravel to be delivered from the builders merchant and when he returned we made coffee and ate some of Joan's delicious home made ginger biscuits. We finished our coffee and Joan and I went off to Medriniac to look for a gas cooker. The sky was so blue and the sun was hot, so we drove with all the windows open. Joan commented at the lack of traffic during our journey along country roads. Perhaps because of this, the sides of the roads were alive with wild flowers and their scent wafting through the open windows - we felt tempted to stop the car and pick a bunch. The countryside was mainly farmland, with lots of black and white cows grazing in the fields. The streets in the villages were almost deserted as we drove through except for a few locals going to the Boulangerie for their bread. We came across our least favourite sign - ROUTE BARREE. Summer had arrived bringing with it as usual, the road repairs. This particular deviation route took us well out of our way and unfortunately, when we eventually reached our destination, the store did not sell cookers. It was not much of a compensation for the wasted journey that Joan was able to purchase some pretty earrings and a necklace - although she thought that it was. When we had finished looking round this store which was a real Alladin's cave, we decided to go to the local supermarket to buy something for lunch, but of course we had forgotten that in France everything closes down between 12noon and 2pm and we were too late. We decided to make do with a fry up, which would not go down well with Les because he was on a diet. However, we all ate the tasty pork and apple burgers we had bought from our English butcher and the fresh eggs from René's free range hens - mostly in our garden. When the shops opened after lunch, we bought food for our evening meal. We aimed to eat by 6pm, which would give us time to go out earlier that evening. After dinner we went on a mystery tour with the lads obviously knowing where they were going, but they kept us in the dark. Our first stop was to see the medieval Chateau Trecesson. This was a picture worthy setting in the evening sunlight, with a Chateau standing in the middle of a lake. It seemed to appear from no-where, almost fairy like and mysterious. It was built in the fourteenth century from red schist with a magnificent gatehouse with corbelled turrets either side. As it was becoming dark there was a sombre feel when looking over the several kilometres of the tree lined now disused drive. It was not difficult to imagine the scenes of horse drawn carriages approaching the Chateau.

After leaving the Chateau, we headed for the large Forêt de Broceliande. This is only a few miles from where we live, but up until this point we had never visited it. This 7,000 hectares forest, is a remaining part of the woodlands that once covered this area of Brittany. Much of it has been replanted since the legendary Arthurian knights roamed here. The poet Chretien de Troyes recounts the Broceliande of ancient legend. Each year, visitors come to explore, hoping to experience a touch of Merlin's magic, or perhaps a fleeting glimpse of the Holy Grail. Within the forest, we stopped at a small village called Paimpont, standing at the centre of the forest and acting as its main resort. It dates only from the revolution, and is most unusual with an enclosed centre of purplish-grey stone houses. Nearby is a large lake glistening in the evening sunlight and not far away is the 11th century abbey church belonging to a monastery that once stood beside the lake. We visited one of the crêperies in the village where we enjoyed a really good brandy with a cup of fresh coffee. We were sitting outside near to an archway in the still evening air, watching the house martins swooping down low to catch flies. We then realised that the street could only be accessed at one end from under this archway.

On our way home through the forest, the heat of the day caused the subsequent falling rain to create a mist visibly rising from the tarmac roads and adding to the mysterious forest scene and stimulating our imagination about the earlier forest dwellers. Our mystery tour turned out to be very enjoyable. We arrived home quite chirpy, perhaps as a result of the brandies which had seemed very strong and burning all the way down to the tummy. The chaps were hungry as is usual, so we had some cheese and biscuits and a hot drink whilst chatting about what we would do the next day before finally retiring to bed.

Dave awoke at 7am and arrived with our cuppa. We breakfasted and Joan volunteered to do the washing up and I would do the toilet run (clean the loos) and bathroom.

Joan and I worked together to prepare lunch and the evening meal. With our chores finished, we walked down to the lake and were both very surprised to hear the noise made by the frogs or toads which we had never heard there before. We came to the conclusion it must be mating time. We were also lucky to see a large heron waiting patiently for some poor fish to appear.

After lunch I introduced Joan to an Intermarché, which is one of the large supermarkets in Ploërmel. Afterwards we went into the town to have a look around. We explored the large sixteenth century church followed by some twentieth century window-shopping. Ploërmel was the scene of a battle between 30 English and 30 French knights in the thirteenth century resulting in a French victory leaving to the imagination how the course of history would have been different had the result gone the other way.

Returning to more mundane matters - we dashed home to cook the evening meal. It was great having Joan around to reduce my workload. That evening we went to visit Mimi at her bar in Taupont and as usual she was pleased to see us and told us about two shops where we could buy a gas cooker.

It rained all that night but by the morning the sun was out. Joan and I went into Taupont church for the 10.30 Mass. It wasn't very different to attending mass at home. Joan said that I would have to tell her what to do. " oh don't worry, it is very like the Church of England" I said. Sadly I thought to myself, Mass was no longer said in Latin. When it was you could go anywhere in the world and understand it. We enjoyed the service and many people made us feel welcome, including the verger, who shook hands with us. That afternoon we sat out in the garden - correction nettle patch - and Joan wrote her cards to England. I had been concerned about her coming and living in our quite primitive conditions but I need not have worried as she was enjoying herself and David was keeping her going with his sense of humour, gathering flowers for her and putting them on her bedside locker. He insisted on calling her `ma petite fleur' (my little flower.)

When Joan wrote her postcards, she was telling everyone how we sat outside for meals and went out every night - anyone would think we were having a ball as in actual fact, we were working very hard, whilst enjoying ourselves when time allowed.

The renovation work was progressing, although causing much dust and disruption with David and Les working non stop between frequent tea breaks. The kitchen tiles were nearly all laid but not without a couple of mishaps but this time it was Joan who damaged the tiles after they had been laid - not me. When we got up the following morning, Dave had put up a sign over the tiles saying ROUTE BAREE, this caused much laughter in particular from the French plumber who wanted to work in the kitchen. The concrete interior windowsills in the bedrooms, were nearly all hardened and it was interesting watching Dave mould them with the sand and cement, into shape and then polish them. Les completed putting up the plasterboard in the stair well, which necessitated much cutting and shaping. Joan and I went for our daily walk going this time across the fields admiring the lovely wild flowers gathering a bunch of what seemed to me to be wild Lavateria to place in the rooms.

The next day we promised ourselves a day off to go to the beach but alas it rained, so we went to the market at Auray. Again our luck was out since the market started early and by the time we arrived at 12 midday, it was finishing. I bought some avocado pears for 1 franc each which was a lot cheaper than England were I pay up to the equivalent of 7.5 francs for each pear. We bought a kilo of freshly picked tomatoes complete with stalks. When we left the market we went down to the port and parked on the breakwater to eat picnic style with cold chicken and salad baguettes and a selection of French cheeses. After lunch, the sun began to come out so we decided to go to Locmariaquer, where we got out of the car to look at the sea and take some photographs. After Carnac, this small oyster port is an important site in Brittany for megaliths.

The hour when the tide is in full flood is the time to visit Locmariaquer. This is when the Atlantic surges into the Golfe de Morbihan, through the narrow channel between this village and Port Navalo. It is an amazing sight to contemplate the enormous power created by the merging of water currents. Nearby is the Pointe de

Kerpenhir where a granite statue of Our Lady of Kerdro standing to protect sailors (Kerdro is Bretagne for safe return)
We walked along the beach to breath in the fresh air, before returning to the car to drive to Quiberon, going via la Trinité-s-Mer, where there is one of the busiest marinas on the coast of Brittany and well known for its oyster breeding beds. We proceeded to Carnac which lies within Quiberon bay and is known throughout the world for its Menhirs (pre-historic standing stones). As we passed through the resort with its sandy beaches, I thought to myself that I would like to spend a holiday there. When we arrived at Quiberon, we stopped at a small cafe overlooking the sea for our ice cream and lemonade.
From our guidebooks we learnt that Quiberon was once an island but is now attached to the mainland by a narrow isthmus.

We did a tour of the local shops and bought some perfume and sun cream. That evening we stayed in to play whist and rummy which was good fun with all the barracking going on. Joan and Dave beat us mercilessly.

The next day I was painting the doors, in between times we went shopping. The electrician called with his father and we paid them their bill, which we thought was very reasonable. David, who is good at woodwork, was busy boxing in pipes and he was making a neat job of it. He explained how he made the wooden handles by first producing a pattern. The handle was to enable access for meter reading, but this was later to become a joke with people mistakenly thinking that it was a snooker cue case and attempting to pick it up.

That evening, the chaps went out on their own, we stayed behind being too exhausted to gad about. Joan did the ironing and I finished the painting. The following day I decided to take Joan to Vannes and the traffic was busier than usual. I was a little concerned, because we had left the map at home and although it was easy getting there, it would be a different story trying to find our way out of the city. We arrived in Vannes and we drove down to the port, found an interesting looking bar where we stopped for a drink. The locals appeared to be drinking pastisse or their brandy chocolate mix - we decided to try the latter. Afterwards we went into the town, browsing round some very up- market shops. Joan purchased some picture post cards and we continued our walk - about around the castle walls and through the `jardins spectacular' as overheard from a French lady when she looked at the flower gardens - we agreed with her that the gardens were truly spectacular.

Eventually, we decided that we should attempt to find our way home with Joan looking a bit anxious - which was nothing to the way I felt. When approaching a filling station I said, "I think we should fill up on diesel, just in case we get lost". Remembering a previous occasion when we had visited Vannes when Les was driving, he had taken the signs to Rennes and then Lorient or so I recalled, so off we went. We found the motorway for Rennes and low and behold it said Ploërmel which we both spotted at the same time and literally shrieked with relief. What a day! Not satisfied with all this tension, when we returned to the house, Les wanted me to go with him to buy the new gas cooker. Our first stop was to a Mobis super store, where there was a plentiful selection of cookers from which to choose. Eventually we decide on a gaz cooker. This was not straight forward as the model we had chosen, was for mains supply gas and had to be converted to bottled gas supply for use in the countryside where there was no piped gas. The lady who sold it to us said, in a most dramatic manner, "it is most important that it is converted or WHOOSH!", by which she meant we would blow up - I think. Les said we would look at the manual (all in french I might add) or ask René, which we did, but he was none the wiser. Back to the shop we go with the cooker the next morning, for them to change the jets for us.

We collected it at 5pm and tried it out but the grill was an enigma - no doubt in time I would work it out. After a further two years I was still trying to do this.

Joan's bedroom was nearly finished with just the decorating to do poor thing - she had been moved out of her room three times in the space of 10 days and each time we had to do a good clean before she could go back in, with the dust from the plaster boarding horrendous. It was the cutting of the board, which made the dust when Dave insisted on cutting it with an angle grinder inside the house. Why he could not cut it outside, I will never know, men are strange, the more dust they create the better they like it. I think I mentioned before the highlight of our day was going to the dustbin since on the way, we meet all and sundry. Bon jour, bon jour, very good for our French and on one such excursion, Hélén our nearby neighbour, stopped us and said in French come in for a drink and something to eat and to meet the new Anglais. I readily accepted the invitation. Joan and I went to her house. Much to our amazement when we arrived, the room was full of people sitting round a large table in the kitchen, eating and drinking. It is strange in French houses you rarely get beyond the kitchen. We sat down to be given wine and snacks. Trying to converse with those sitting around the table we had difficulty since there were two Peruvians from Lima, who spoke Spanish and a little French, one child who spoke Spanish but could also speak French, four French people and two other English. We were introduced to our compatriots, Edith and Peter, who were both very friendly and both could speak French. They were retired schoolteachers. Peter had taught mathematics but I am not sure what his wife had taught. I talked with them as did Joan, but Hélén kept interrupting and saying everyone must speak in French, so we did just that. It was great fun and Joan was drinking the Ricard like no tomorrow. This before had caught me, so I was careful to dilute mine with water. Joan was as happy as Larry all day. When we were due to leave, Edith and Peter asked us round in the evening to see their house. That evening however, we had invited some of our French friends for drinks and a bite to eat, so we asked Edith and Peter to join us first and we could go to their house afterwards. This was agreed and everyone would be at Pre du Lac at 6pm.

Yvonne our immediate neighbour often left us some goodies by the back door, when she had been working in her garden, depending on what was in season. This time we had salad and lots of cherries from which I made several cherry pies and crumbles.

One evening we all dressed in our finery, to go to the Salle de Fete in Ploërmel. Mimi told us they were playing English music. Well you could have fooled me, it was folk type music but certainly not English. It was a foot tapping rhythm with musicians who could certainly play the violins and the Breton bagpipes. Dave the Scot informed me, that it was not the same as the Scottish bagpipes. I wanted to tell Dave a story I had been told by my music teacher but thought better of it, but I will tell it now. A renowned composer was talking to a group of musicians and they were discussing bagpipes. He said the bagpipe is the only instrument I know that when you have finished learning how to play it, the sound is just like that when you have just begun to learn to play the instrument. The evening was a great success with everyone getting up to dance, except us. We were not sure what to do, so we sat and watched, with our feet tapping out the rhythms which were not unlike the Irish river dance music. The rhythms were much slower and large circles of dancers kept in contact by linking their little fingers. It reminded me of line dancing and Dave was determined that he was going to learn the dancing and he said he would be taking his dancing shoes with him on the next trip. The hall was large and there must have been at least 400 people of all ages there. It was interesting to see how well behaved all the young people were. Even with a bar there, no one over indulged. We departed around 11pm and we heard the next day that it went on until 2.30 am.

The evening we invited our friends round was a great success, with the conversation all in French with the help of the dictionary. After the others had gone, we walked with Edith and Peter to their house at the other end of the hamlet. It was an interesting house but totally different to ours. It was more modern and only decoration of the rooms being required. I was envious but I wouldn't really want to swop since ours had such character and when the work was completed it would look part of the traditional countryside. We sat out on their veranda overlooking the very large garden fully stocked with flowers and I could not help making comparisons with our nettle patch. The men drank more wine and beer but I settled for a good English cuppa and we talked until late. On their land there was an old barn and Peter was eager to ask Les what he thought of it and if it could be converted to a gîte. Les thought the structure was sound the stonework and the roof were good and it had a lot of possibilities. They thought we were very brave taking on what we had, although the light was now beginning to show at the end of our tunnel. With the progress we had made on the first house a further two trips would see it finished - hopefully. We left them at around 11pm promising to meet up again later in the year, exchanging addresses and saying our farewells.

Our stay in France was drawing to a close. Joan didn't want to go home, but she agreed to go on the proviso that she could return on our next trip. It had so reminded her of her days in Africa, with the corn now all golden brown and the hot sun. She could see the similarities between our house and living in a Rondavel, which was an African house, made from mud and wattle with dirt floors and a thatched roof. I think that the dust in our house reminded her of the Rondavel in Africa where there was so much of it. She told me she used to polish the furniture with shoe polish because she was unable to buy furniture polish out there. When Joan qualified as a state registered nurse she went out to Africa in the Colonial Nursing Service in the late forties and whilst nursing there, she met and married her husband who had been one of her patients in the local hospital. With our return imminent, I decided to clean the car and removed Les's two walking sticks and placed them on the roof rack whilst I cleaned inside the car. After this I drove to the supermarket and what happened to those two sticks is a mystery since they were never seen again. Les was furious blaming me saying that I was such a scatter brain, poor Joan got out of the way quick and later she said to me " well I can see his point" " Yes " I said "but don't let him hear you say it".

When René heard about the lost walking sticks, he produced a very old Charlie Chaplin type of cane for Les to use. The cane had more than its share of woodworm and despite the wire binding we put on, it quickly collapsed.

When we were making room in the outbuilding / shed, we uncovered an old bicycle in a very bad state. Les asked René, if he would enter on it in the Tour de France. We were unsure whether his rejection of the idea was based on his condition or that of the bike. We also discovered sickles, cast iron cooking pots with legs, flat irons and other unusual hooks and tools that could be cleaned and painted. There were also items of old pottery, worth keeping including what seemed to be an urn needing some restoration. That night we had just turned off the light and our little friend Belle the dog started to howl when a voice from the next room in a broad Scottish accent, shouted out just like a sergeant major, SHUT UP and she did just that.

The next morning Joan and I packed the car and the men finished off odd jobs whilst we went down to the super markets to buy last minute goodies, to take home. We did all the washing of the bedding, got it dried and put away. We departed at 4.30pm and the journey was pleasant, stopping a couple of times on the way. The boat we were sailing back on, was the Pride of Cherbourg, which was certainly more comfortable than the boat we came out on. Alas the sleeping arrangements were not comfortable, without cabins due to our unavoidable late booking because of the water in the diesel problem. The couchettes we had to use instead, were not easy to sleep in, although, I did sleep quite well but Joan didn't and the chaps dozed on and off and we were glad when it was time for breakfast. Another trip nearly over, with only the car journey to Worcester to endure.

CHAPTER TEN

Peaches with Everything

We travelled from Portsmouth to Cherbourg on the Super Star Express in September 1999. This necessitated getting up at 3am to depart Kempsey at 3.30am. We arrived at Portsmouth just in time for the boat departure at 7am. The man directing the flow of traffic onto the boat complained because we were late in arriving. Les has a disabled persons badge due to osteo-arthritis and therefore we should arrive early, so that we can be placed in a suitable position to use the lift when we get on board. Our journey to Portsmouth was accompanied by a noise, which was unfamiliar to us. We had a window frame that May had given us tied to the roof rack. When the wind got under it the sound was like that of the washboard in the old skiffle groups. Dave got out of the car and secured the fastening ropes, which solved the problem. Oh! I almost forgot, Les pulled up very quickly to avoid a parking car and the frying pan, which we had packed on the top of everything else in the back of the car, nearly decapitated Joan. The boat was larger than we thought it would be and was certainly much quicker than the normal ferries. The journey took two and three quarter hours and the crossing was calm. We wandered into the various shops on board and Les bought tobacco for Ruth. Joan and I went outside on deck it was very breezy and the smell of the fumes from the engines forced us to return inside. We had some better than usual coffee from the cafeteria to help us pass the time and arrived in Cherbourg at 9.45 English time.

We drove down as far as Ste - Mére Eglise where we stopped for a picnic in one of the customary designated table and chairs places. I had packed roast beef sandwiches made with the beef from a roast I had cooked the previous day. Whilst we were eating the sandwiches, someone asked what had happened to the horseradish sauce. I retorted that we were to make do with English mustard, tomatoes and crisps and washed down with flask coffee - there is always one difficult to please.

We arrived in Quelneuc at 4.30pm French time and Dave proceeded to turn on the water and electricity. We all helped unpack the car. After a drink Joan and I started to clean the dust off from everywhere. I must admit the house is getting cleaner as the dust is now only on the top surfaces. We ate our pork and apple burgers from our local butcher in England, with scrambled eggs, toast and beans. What a mixture! Followed by treacle tart and custard for a quick fix.

As this was September, the peach tree in the garden was loaded with peaches, just ripe with a lovely rosy hue to their skins - delicious to eat. With this plentiful harvest - it was peaches with everything. Dave who says can do most things including cooking, said he would do the sweet for us on one of the evenings. He sliced the peaches then added water and sugar and heated them until the sugar caramalised. He added a generous amount of brandy and flambéed them and when served with lashings of crème frêche, tasted marvellous.

After we had eaten, we went for a walk by the lake. The air was still and the temperature warm. This time it was quiet with no frogs or toads courting. Les in the meantime went off to speak with a recommended decorator at the other end of the village. When we returned, Joan and I made up the beds and we all retired early at 10pm.

The following morning we measured all the floor areas of the two other houses we had bought. The purpose of this exercise was for Les to draw up plans for planning permission to renovate these houses.

On Thursday, Les and I went to see the Notaire but we could not think what the word for appointment was, it turned out to be as obvious as `rendezvous'. This we made for the following Wednesday. We went to the Tax Office to pay the bill for the Tax Fonciere, which is the regional portion of our council tax bill for the house. This went without a hitch. When we returned Joan had coffee ready with some of her home made ginger biscuits which she kept a watchful eye on otherwise they would be all eaten at one sitting by David. Joan and I went to do some food shopping at LeClerc supermarket for our lunch.

In the afternoon, I decided to try and get accustomed to my new cooker. I am so used to cooking with electricity, I find gas most strange. I decided to cook some scones for tea and they turned out well enough for them to soon disappear from the plate.

I made a steak pie for supper and Joan busied herself with the endless ironing. When we had finished our chores, we decided to have another look at our new English friend's house. There was no one at the house and we assumed that they had returned to England since it was deserted with everything securely shuttered up. Returning by the lake we picked some blackberries on the way. Joan found an apple tree which we proceeded to shake and managed to get three apples but the others fell into the ditch which we were not prepared to retrieve worrying about the possibility of treading on an unsuspecting snake as we were only wearing sandals. We would send Dave out later for them in his big boots. On our way back we met Hélén and chatted to her in our modest French - she was well and able to bring us up to date on a few local happenings.

That evening was warm enough to tempt us to have our meal outside which we always enjoy because we rarely have the opportunity in England.

Les was getting ready for the decorator to arrive to provide us with a quotation for plastering and decorating the whole house.

Monsieur le painter arrived accompanied by his granddaughter. He spoke only French but his granddaughter did speak a little English. They looked around the house making comments here and there. I choose the colours for the paint and emulsion. They went away with the understanding they would let us have a quote for the work on the next Friday. That evening we went to the popular local bar in Ploërmel where we were recognised immediately and the owner was very chatty with us. I think they liked to practice English on us. The next day was Friday and we had been told that there was a market in Ploërmel. Our friend Dave awaked us with an early cup of tea and as soon as breakfast was finished, Joan and I departed for the market. We found it, after I had obtained directions from one of the locals. It was behind the large church in the main square, which left us wondering how we had come to miss it on past visits. The stalls were mainly selling fish, meats, vegetables, bread and confectionery. There was also the customary rotisserie cooking chickens and bacon joints, with their distinctive aromas. I purchased some vegetables, fruit and a baguette, which were all cheaper than buying at the supermarket. "Bon marché," we thought.

At the fruit stall I gave the man too much money and he went to great lengths to attempt to tell me the amount he wanted. Thankfully a gentleman came to my rescue, speaking very good English and helping me to understand. Everyone seemed to be so helpful and very honest. I have trouble sorting out the centimes but I am now OK with the francs.

After lunch that day, we cleared out one of the bedrooms which had until now been used as a workshop. All the tools and the spare wood and plasterboard were transferred into the end house. The room was now clear for the decorator to fill the plaster boarding joints and to plaster and decorate in there. My job to clean the floor was a marathon. Again I was thinking that if only these men would put a dustsheet down, it would save so much time and hard work scraping off the dried plaster.

Some time ago Hélén told us that a couple had bought the property opposite us. This house was also for renovation. The owners were Irish, with a German contract builder, doing the renovation for them. Conversation in French with a German was very difficult for nosey English people. Needless to say we had not found out very much as to what was happening with this house during our previous visits. On this trip we noticed two people working in the garden and Les went over to introduce himself. The couple were the parents of the owners and they were just there doing odd jobs like clearing the garden. Their daughter and her husband also owned a house in Redon, which they let out as a gîte. That evening the parents came over to us for a drink and we found out that they were both retired. The man had worked in the aircraft industry and his wife had been in the army. We enjoyed a very pleasant evening and we were pleased to have their family as neighbours. The following day they left for Devon to have a week's holiday on their way home. They live in Northern Ireland and we asked them about the troubles. They said "you are always aware of it obviously but you just have to get on with your life."

That evening when everyone had gone, I put on the French language tapes since we were all so eager to improve our French, but as the saying goes "the spirit is willing but the flesh is weak". Dave's eyes began to look glassy and it was all he could do to keep awake, so off to bed he went and we soon followed - so much for the French tapes. On Saturday we had a busy day scrubbing floors and changing bedrooms around. Our bedroom is now the one previously occupied by Dave who swopped for the single room which was used for storing the tools. With all the floors clean, Joan and I put the covers on the four-piece suite, which up until now had been kept hidden away. Now that the plaster boarding was all but complete, the amount of dust had reduced drastically. In the evening we all went out to La Gacilly which is a pretty town with lots of small cafés. At the top end of the town was a water mill and stream with a small bridge over it. La Gacilly is a village of character, relying on the sales of its many arts and crafts for a living and the town's development has been helped by the local Yves Rocher whose name is famous in the cosmetics industry.

Because it was late when we set out, by the time we arrived at La Gacilly, it was dusk so we decided to return to Quelneuc and visit Mimi's bar. Mimi was all excited about her recent trip to America where she had thoroughly enjoyed staying with her niece and she was continuously saying, "have a nice day"

On Sunday Joan and I went to Mass where both priests and several people I had previously met there welcomed us. Following Mass we went across the road to a very tempting patisserie. We do not go there very often because they are expensive but their cakes are a dream. Joan said she was going to treat us all to a custard slice to eat with our coffee when we got back.

Lunch was eaten outside again, as the weather was just right- not too hot. Afterwards we went down to the phone booth by the man made beach. I had been trying to contact Dee and Fran at their new house in Wales to arrange when they were coming to stay. However, Dee had given me the wrong code and when I showed it to Les, he realised the mistake and he remembered the code from when he lived in Wales. I kept my fingers crossed and tried dialling the new code which worked. Dee said he was sorry but they would not be visiting us on this trip because they were not returning to France until the day after we had left because his car had to go into the garage to rectify steering trouble.

Later that day Yvonne arrived with more peaches which she said were apricots, but they looked very much like peaches to me and I made a tasty crumble. Dave went to the area around the lake and picked more blackberries - I must say on this visit we were inundated with fruit. Joan and I went for our daily walk picking some wild flowers for the vase. In the evening we ate roast duck and Les complained because I had not made any plum sauce. For sweet we had home made peach jelly and mountains of crême frêche. That evening we stayed in and played dominoes 5's and 3's Laugh! We were in fits - none of us had laughed so much for a long time and really it was all about nothing, although I suspect it was something to do with the quantity of vin rouge. When we were getting ready for bed, we noticed the large number of flies in the house and Dave got out the Vapona spray, using it on everything that moved. By the time Dave had finished, we were nearly all suffering as much as the flies.

On the Monday, René came to discuss the purchase of the land with Les and before this I had pursuaded Les to keep a little more than he had previously suggested. René seemed pleased with the outcome and we went to see the official land surveyor who deals with marking out of land for sale and authorised him to liaise with René to mark out the boundary posts.

Later that day we went to Auray which is an ancient town built on the banks of the River Loch and is famous in Breton history for the battle fought under its walls in 1364 ending the war of succession in which Jean de Montford was victorious. Cadoudal from Auray who tried to kidnap him confronted Napoleon in Paris but Cadoudal was arrested, executed and his remains put in a tomb near his family home in Auray.

In 1776 Benjamin Franklin landed here on his way to seek the help of King Louis XVI with the American war of independence. It is reputed that Auray is the last place that Julius Caesar reached in his conquest of Western France. The old harbour area has some fifteenth century houses and a schooner reconstructed with information about life during the nineteenth century.

The sun was out in the busy market and we all bought something. I bought a sweater for Penny my daughter-in-law, Dave bought some jeans and Les bought some foam packing - but he would not say what it was for.

Towards lunchtime we had a coffee in the market and we noticed a stall with a rôtisserie where they were cooking chickens which smelt appetising. We decided to buy one for our lunch and have it picnic style with two baguettes, some tomatoes and a couple of melons. We left the market and set off for Le Pouldu, which is a charming seaside resort at the mouth of the Laïta with splendid beach backed by cliffs. It became famous a hundred years ago when the painter Paul Gauguin settled there with a few friends. At this time of year it was lovely with a beautiful beach which was almost deserted, except for a few locals collecting mussels. We parked the car at the top of the cliffs and luckily there were two benches so one we used for preparing the picnic and sat on the other. The picnic was a little primitive with no plates but we did have a kitchen roll that we used instead of plates. Dave dissected the chicken but don't ask how. We split the two baguettes into four and placed the pieces of chicken in the middle. The tomatoes were ripe and juicy and tasted good. When Les took a bite it squirted down the front of his clean shirt. For sweet, we cut the melon, which was a little over ripe, but no one complained.

Afterwards we went on the beach where I had a paddle and then Joan and I wandered round the rock pools, looking at the sea life and found several sea anemones, the odd crab, limpets, cockles and plenty of mussels. It was sufficiently interesting for us to stay there for the whole day. It was so relaxing just to laze in the sun and feel the sand under our feet watching the sea constantly changing. I love the sea and miss it so much since it always reminds me of my younger days when I lived in the Isle of Wight. When we returned home, the lads went for a drink but Joan and I stayed in and played scrabble. On the Wednesday, Joan and I again drove to Mèdriniac where we wanted to see the price of carpets at the local store that we had visited on our previous trips. A large carpet for in front of the fireplace was £60. I would compare this when I returned home with English prices. We browsed around the store and Joan bought me a container for holding my large cooking utensils enabling me to find them when they are required.

We went to the planning office in the Hôtel de Ville, Taupont in the afternoon to submit the applications for the changes we wanted to make to the structure of the second and third properties we had bought. We were happy to say on this occasion that we got everything right first time - or so we thought.

In the evening we went to the Irish Pub and to our surprise, it had a new landlord who was younger and the clientele were also younger and it was certainly busier. We did feel disappointed to lose our friendly bar man. The next day we went into Ploërmel to shop for the supplies and presents we would be taking home. These were mainly spirits, wine and chocolate. I always buy some of the French butter which is more like the butter we used to have in England rather than the present day supermarket processed product and of course, their coffee which is cheaper than ours and tastes better.

Dave went out early that morning to help René plough for one hour he really enjoyed gaining some experience of the new, very large tractor.

That evening we were invited to René's house for drinks and little bites to eat. These events are now becoming more vocal with our French certainly improving. I was more at ease and not being so nervous, I could communicate much better. When we first arrived, Alfred and Yvonne were at the house, but they departed early and when they had gone, René asked if we would like to look around his house and of course, we said " yes". The house was quite different to

English houses. The main room was very large with a beautiful polished table in the centre and more like the size of a boardroom table, in England. Either side of it was a bench, highly polished, matching the table. Not one easy chair anywhere in sight - maybe this is why the French do not have so many back problems as the English do. At the far end of the room, was the kitchen area with all the units expensively finished and all appliances hidden behind decorative wooden doors. There was an array of cupboards all in the same highly polished wood. The pictures on the walls were very interesting showing the house and the farm through the generations up to the present day. Everywhere was so tidy and spotlessly clean. The ground floor was all tiled, as was the stairs up to the first floor.

On leaving the main room, we were shown the wine store that was full of many varieties of wines with respective age markings. The central heating equipment was also viewed and René proudly explained its workings to us. There was a granary that was empty but could easily be converted to make two good bedrooms. Trust me I am so used to looking at property with the idea of restoring it, when I see any spare space I imagine what could be done with it. We proceeded upstairs into the first bedroom where I let out a gasp when I saw the massive bed which was beautifully designed in very old hard wood that had been kept polished over the years. The carving on the bed head was most impressive. The wardrobe matched the bed and its hinges were so different to ours since they were patterned and the wood was carved to match the carving on the bed-head. On the other side of the room was a settle that I would judge to be about the same period. René could see my interest and he said "not for sale". We laughed and proceeded to René's bedroom that was modern in comparison but again very sparsely furnished - just the bed, a television and one upright chair. I asked him if he did the cleaning he said " no! a lady comes each week to clean". The floors were all highly polished and no curtains since there were shutters to the windows. We went along to René's office which was all very tidy. There was a desk with a computer on it, a chair and a cupboard. We were shown the bathroom that was like ours. We talked at length about the house and we were interested in its origins. We learnt from René that the farm had been in the family for many generations and had changed and developed over the years into its present day modern activities. We discussed the mechanisation of the farm and its implications. When I looked at the time, it was nearly 10 pm and I was thinking we should be leaving because I know René gets up just after 5am because we hear the milking machines go on. So we bid goodnight, thanking him for a most enjoyable evening. It was still quite warm outside and the sky was full of stars and when we reached the house there was some kind of movement, but Dave was first in because he had the keys since he was fed up with me and Les loosing them. We got inside and low and behold there was the biggest toad I have ever seen on the doorstep looking at us. I quickly went into the bathroom and got the long mop which had a fair amount of bleach on it and hoped this would see him off - not a bit of it.

The toad just got up on the side of the doorframe and I pushed him with the mop but he refused to move. I was not brave enough to handle him, so eventually Dave came to the rescue and picked him up and placed him outside.

He seems to like our garden because I have seen him a couple of times since then and heard his croaking.

The next morning I awoke with a hangover which must have been the Ricard from the night before. That day Joan and I made ready the house for Bertrand the estate agent to visit and give his opinion on the renovation work that we had done so far. He was late in arriving and Les had gone with Dave to buy their wine for taking home. So I was left to show Bertrand around the house. I explained Les wanted to know if we were doing the right things. Bertrand appeared to be impressed commenting on how much bigger the house looked compared with what he could remember from the time when we purchased it. He said he would like to come again when it was completed and in the meantime, he would think about its sale value. He apologised for being late and said he would visit in November and speak with Les because by then the decorating would be finished. Before he departed he said he now had a son called William and said he could now have a rest. He was obviously very proud of his new baby. That evening we had the neighbours in for our usual pre departure drinks and bites to eat and to bid our farewells until the next time.

      The next day we were up very early in time to reach Cherbourg for 11 am. I had packed sandwiches so we stopped on the way for a snack and a drink of coffee. We arrived at the port in plenty of time, to be met by one of the ferry staff who told us that our Super Star Express boat had been cancelled because the gales were force eight. The Super Star Express cannot sail in rough seas, but all was not lost. They had booked us on the Pride of Bilbau, which I had sailed on before to Spain and it was a very large boat - sturdy as a rock. However, this did not leave until 1 pm. This gave us time to look round the port and have a cup of tea, before it was time to embark. Joan and I made sure to take our sea legs since we were a little uneasy to say the least at the prospect of the trip ahead of us. We need not have worried since the return journey was great and the boat was steady and none of us suffered seasickness. We arrived home thinking to ourselves that it had been a good trip with all the work on schedule. Our next trip was planned for November 1999 preferably from Portsmouth to Caen.

CHAPTER ELEVEN

Quelneuc not Carnac

We arrived at Quelneuc at 6.45 pm, in the dark. What a treat it was when we opened the front door and found the house was how we had left it - all clean and tidy and virtually dust free. We did find some soot in the fireplace that had been blown down the chimney by the severe winds and rain. We set to work removing the plastic covers from the furniture. In our absence our little four legged friends, the wee mouses had been having a ball over my three-piece suite and to top it all had left their calling cards, so action had to be taken. On the top of my shopping list had to be vermin exterminator and Les promised to fill the remaining mouse entrance holes. Joan and I were really pleased with ourselves because we were actually sitting down and eating a hot meal within one hour of arrival. This time our beds felt very cold and so out came the hot water bottles and within a short time we had the beds made up complete with the hot bottles. We lit the gaz fire and put on the central heating - the latter consisting of one electric radiator in the lounge. On the landing we put an electric fan heater and surprisingly the house very quickly became warm. Yvonne popped over to welcome us and to ask after our journey. I always find it difficult at first to get into the other language, but after a cup of coffee with her and listening to her report on the health of the locals, I began to relax and consequently my French improved. After she left, we decided it was bed early for everyone. I think Joan and I were tired after our umpteenth tour on foot round the deck of the boat, since Joan has a thing about walking and does so whenever there is any opportunity. I quickly fell asleep and it seemed only a moment before Dave arrived with the morning cup of tea. I got up and prepared breakfast of egg, bacon and tomatoes. It is unusual to have a cooked breakfast but as it was cold I thought it would give the men a good start for the day. Dave was replacing the old original front door that was going to be a big job. The doors on the properties we have bought, are much wider than those at home. We had ordered special tongued and groved hard wood in the UK to save time for Dave to make the door in Quelneuc. The door took three days to finish but it had not been straightforward. When the wood panels were assembled they were still 3 centimetres too narrow for the doorframe, so Dave had to find some timber to bridge the gap. Eventually the door was finished and it blended well with the stonework of the house. On our first day Joan and I went to do some food shopping and whilst we were away, our English friends, Peter and Edith had visited. On this occasion our visit to France coincided with theirs. Les invited them over in the evening for drinks and a snack. We were pleased to see Edith and Peter again and they brought us up to date on the village gossip. Edith had just passed her A level in French and they were here to do some decoration to their house and they wanted us to go over and view their work later in the week. It was a good excuse to meet up again since it is always relaxing to talk with some English friends after struggling with the French language.

We received some disappointing news the painter and decorator informed us he was unable to start until December. Les was not happy about this, since we had hoped to finish the work on the house after the decorator had done his work and this would delay the completion for another month. Unfortunately it was not always possible to understand what the decorator was saying and in the translation of words some of the meaning got lost or misinterpreted. I understood that his mother was ill, and this was the reason for the delay in starting. He then said that the plaster boarding was not yet suitable to plaster skim and he would not start until it was. To further complicate matters, he said he would give us another quote. We decided to ask René to interpret for us at a meeting arranged for the following evening. Les was getting anxious because we wanted to put this house on the market and time was going on. The meeting took place but still we were none the wiser. We decided to talk with Mimi and ask her if she could recommend a painter and decorator /plasterer. We discussed this at length with her, and she did tell us that he had quoted for her to decorate her house but she had not given him the work because he was too expensive. Mimi said she knew of English plasterer called Lee, whose wife regularly shopped in her mini - market and she gave his telephone number to Les. That evening we all stayed in except for Les he was going to tell our original decorator that we would not be asking him to do the work.

For dinner I prepared chilli con carne with which I like rice but Les always likes mashed potato. David suggested putting the rice in with the chilli and adding some wine allowing the rice to absorb the chilli and the wine, saying that it would taste good. I had my doubts but we gave it a try and it turned out to be edible. Later that evening it was the England v Scotland football match and so we listened to it on the radio, as we do not have the luxury of a TV. When Scotland scored a goal David was very happy. The following morning David overslept which is most unusual and Les went down first to make the tea. We had breakfast and set to work in earnest. David was tightening up some of the plasterboards and Les was fixing internal hard wood facings with the elm wood bought over from England. I was grouting the kitchen floor - what a job - no wonder no one wanted to do it, I soon found out why. When the kitchen floor was grouted I had a touch of housemaid's knee. I then began staining the parts of the beams left exposed on the upper floor, but before I could actually stain them they had to be cleaned up and I quickly put on a mask to prevent inhalation of the dust and dirt. The vacuum cleaner came in useful to reach into the nooks and crannies to remove all the dust, straw and dead insect remains that had accumulated over the last two hundred years on the top off the walls. After cleaning, I applied the stain to the beam-ends and they began to look so much better, as if they were at last being cared for. The next day Les was still cutting the elm wood with which he had been filling in the holes beside the beams and David was tiling the floor of the entrance by the new front door. This was difficult because the door well was a step lower than the rest of the floor level.

Later in the day Les went to the planning office in Taupont, to discuss the plans for alterations which were needed for the next two houses, since we had received a letter stating Dossier Incomplet for the plans submitted. Joan and I went to do some shopping at the local market. We had decided to have fish and chips for lunch. I had asked Fran when I had met up with her in the U.K. what the word for cod was and she said it was moureau. In French I asked for four pieces of cod, but they said they had sold out. Not to be daunted we went to a fish shop in town where I followed the same procedure. The man did not understand me so I said "cod anglais", "Ah oui, Madame" and he produced the four steaks of cod, costing £10 after conversion from the French franc - needless to say I would not be returning. Joan offered to cook the meal. Well, it was the strangest piece of cod I have ever eaten. I am sure it was merlan, or something similar. Its texture was more like swordfish. The taste was so strong and the bones were as big as tooth picks. Joan in her usual economic way had cut the top half of the fillets to eat that day, the tail ends she had saved for a fish pie the next day. I would not be having the fish pie that was for sure and I settled for scrambled eggs that day, but everyone else enjoyed the fish pie, mind you they eat anything I had come to the conclusion. That evening we went down to the local bar for a drink.

We discovered that it was Nouveau Beaujolais day, which is a celebration day for the current year's vintage. The bar staff was in traditional dress. We were offered the wine which the men accepted but Joan and I asked for cognac and a cafe grand with cream, much to the dismay of the waiter, who wanted us to try his wine. The people in the bar were in a festive mood and very talkative with one of the French men asking us where we were from and we replied Quelneuc. He mistakenly, as a result of our pronunciation, thought we had said Carnac. He appeared to be most impressed since Carnac is one of the most expensive marina resorts in Brittany. He asked if we had a grand bateau in the marina there. Rubbing his thumb and finger together he said "trés riche". We were more than a little confused until Les realised the mistake and pronounced Quelneuc more precisely. The man then recognised where we meant, pulled a few centimes from his pocket and said, " pour votre charité". Everyone understood his quick sense of humour. It transpired that he had worked in England when he was younger as a waiter. This had given him a good command of the English language. The evening passed quickly and we said good night to our friends saying we would meet up later in the week.

The next day I continued staining the beams and Joan did the catering. By the afternoon I was beginning to get a headache from the fumes. Joan and I decided enough was enough and we would go for a long walk to clear our heads. The weather was mild and the sun was shining so we went down to the lake where there is always something to see such as birds, fish, the odd frog and on occasion, the odd person as Joan was to find out at a later date. Today it was deserted but it is always refreshing to go to the lake and just look at the water and breath in the fresh air. That evening we went to the house of Peter and Edith. They had been very busy decorating. Their lounge is much smaller than ours is but they had made it look clean and bright with the one wall coloured terra cotta, the other three walls pink and the ceiling white.

Quelneuc not Carnac

Carnac not Quelneuc

When they had bought the house the furnishings had been included in the asking price which apparently often happens in France. It was interesting to see what had been left behind. Some of the furnishings were quite reasonable but others were not to our taste or theirs. We were quite amazed to hear they had been left a usable motor bike amongst their acquisitions. We drank red wine and later we had coffee with homemade barra breidd (welsh). They are entertaining company and the evening was most enjoyable. Their friends in the hamlet tend to differ from ours due to the initial contacts they made when purchasing their house. This means that we have lots of news about the village folk to exchange when we meet with each other and this gives us more knowledge of the local people. Peter had arranged for a plasterer to visit us on Monday, which might have been helpful - if he had turned up. They were returning to the UK on Saturday but would be back in January, so we said that we hoped we would be meeting up again in the new year. We left around 11pm and Dave was still up having stayed behind because he had a headache. He had been listening to my tapes of Pavorotti - I did not see how this could have helped the headache.

The next day we went to the supermarket and bought David 12 bottles of wine to take home since it is so much cheaper in France. In the afternoon we had visitors - René, Robert the contractor and Yvonne. The vin rouge flowed and arrangements were made for Robert to take Les to pay for the materials so that he could install a new fosse septique for the other houses. Since there were more jobs than we had anticipated and time was running out, we decided to remain a few extra days, to ensure that the house would be ready for sale by January 2000. Because the plasterer had let us down, David and I said we would have a go at plastering the small bedroom and see what it turned out like. In for a penny in for a pound, we were beginning to learn that when doing up old properties in France, you have to be prepared to do a lot yourselves and be very flexible. What you start out with as a plan, can change a dozen times before it reaches fruition. Local tradesmen were proving somewhat unreliable as far as arrival dates although some of this we found could be due to misunderstanding of the language but this seemed to be giving them too much of the benefit of the doubt.

The weather was very cold and unless you were working, it was difficult to keep warm. Joan was feeling cold but she did not complain. What had pleased me about this visit, was that we were becoming very friendly with the neighbours - nothing seemed too much trouble and they really had been most helpful. I thanked René for all the assistance he had given us and his reply was simply "we are friends" which said it all to me, so my comment to the people who always criticise the French is "we have only found them kind and helpful". The next day it rained but the work continued. I now had the floor tiles to grout by the new front door. After this was finished, I was asked by Dave to put a lick of paint on the door hinges. He had sanded down the old original hinges and all they needed was a coat of black paint. When I was doing this, Joan decided to go for a walk by the lake and I said to her "now don't go off with any strange men". She had been gone about half an hour and she returned, looking very disconcerted. She said that she had just reached the turning point that takes you to the lake when a car pulled up along side her and continued to crawl along beside her, as she walked. Joan stopped expecting him to drive on but he did not. He pulled the window down and grinned at her but did not speak. Joan said he behaved most oddly, so she looked at him and glared and said in her best french " non!" and at this he took off. She said, " I am sure he was a flasher".

The next day we waited in for the plasterer, recommended by Mimi, to arrive but no such luck. In the evening Les went to telephone him and he said he had been to look for our house but could not find it. I am not surprised because there are no numbers or road names and it is quite amazing how mail or anyone finds us. It was arranged for him to come the next day at 2pm.

The following morning we set out early for the market at Auray. We were very lucky, as on this occasion, all of us were able to purchase Christmas presents to take home. I bought 3 pairs of gloves but unfortunately I lost one pair and I suspect that I left it on the market stall by mistake. I bought two handbags and a woollen suit. Les bought a nice thick cardigan and a coat. Dave bought a cardigan and some presents for his grandchild. Joan bought some pretty china pots. When our shopping was finished, Les went up to the rôtisserie and bought a piece of pork. I bought a couple of baguettes and as usual, we had not come prepared for a picnic but this did not deter the men. " but we haven't a knife to cut the meat" I said. " don't worry" said Dave " my daughter needs some sharp knives for Christmas so I will buy her a set and we can slip one out and use it to cut the meat, wash it and pop it back". That is what we did. We parked in our usual place by the estuary at Auray and luckily that morning, I had prepared a flask of coffee so we were able to have a hot drink. This went down well with the hot pork baguettes making a tasty cheap lunch. When you think we had gone into a bistro and just ordered 4 coffee and it had cost over a fiver. I suppose we were paying for the ambience. When we arrived back home, I needed to telephone my friend May, back in the U.K. She is a neighbour who looks after our house and cat when we are away. She needed to know we were staying on a little longer. After the call I returned home and the plasterer had arrived.

His name is Lee and he is a pleasant young Englishman. He had bought his young son with him of 18 months and Joan proceeded to keep him amused while Lee looked at the work we required. He promised to return the next day with the quote and if we accepted it he would start work on the following Wednesday and continue working in our absence.

That evening Dave cooked the chicken curry and for sweet he made caramelised pears, which he had bought on the market. We all said it was a treat, especially with the vin rouge. Our spirits began to rise now we had at last managed to get some plastering help. I felt tired after our busy day, mainly because Belle, the farm dog, had kept me awake with her barking most of the previous night due again to the full moon. After our meal we all retired to bed.

Hélén, one of our other neighbours, had been in hospital we learnt from Edith, with a woman's complaint, but she was now back home and making a good recovery. The following afternoon, I bought Hélén some flowers at the local garden centre. Joan and I went to her house, which is across the road from ours to give them to her, and we were received with open arms. We were asked to sit down and two large glasses of what I think was port were placed before us, followed by some fancy biscuits and we remained talking for over an hour. Later Hélén's husband Alfred, who is a very friendly quiet man, joined us. When we left Joan commented on the sparse furnishings and she also had noticed that Hélén had been drinking some kind of hot chocolate out of a chipped cup. It was also a little on the cold side in their house. However I thought to myself they may not have much in the way of possessions but they were willing to share with us what little they had and in their simple way they appeared so happy and I thought to myself possessions are not important - it is people that matter. I think Joan was surprised at the austerity of their homes.

That evening we were all sat round the fire, talking over what jobs we would do the following day. Hopefully Dave was going to fill in the gaps at each side of the new front door which would get rid of the draught, once and for all also preventing access for passing mice.

The next day Lee arrived to give us the quote for his work. It came to £700 compared with £2000 for our previous decorator's quote, although the latter included painting the walls and ceilings - so Mimi had been right about him being expensive. Lee would do the plastering and I would be left to decorate, but Les needed time to think about it before he would tell Lee he had the job.   When we had visited Auray Les had bought two tapes one was Irish tunes and the other Scottish reels. David informed me it was not true Scottish music it was Breton music - very similar to the Scottish music. I realised that the beat was the same as the music we had listened to at the salle de féte when we watched the Breton dancing. There was one tune on the Scottish tape I could not help humming I knew that I remembered it from somewhere and eventually it came to me that it was Flower of Scotland, played at the beginning of the rugby matches, between England and Scotland. The days were so full and went so fast and thankfully the weather had improved and we were outside with just our jumper and trousers on which, in November, is not bad. We also got all the washing dry which was a real bonus.

It was Wednesday and Les had arranged to collect the mechanical floor-sanding machine from the hire firm.

David would be sanding two and a half bedroom floors and the upstairs landing. The work was dusty and tiring and Dave had to wear a mask although there was a dust bag on the machine, lots of dust escaped. When the middle bedroom was sanded I set about staining the floorboards which was far from easy and I started with a brush, then I changed to a rag and finally I used a sponge, but I was not happy with the finished result. In part my husband was to blame but he will never admit it, because he was anxious to finish everything, he started on the far side of the same room but no two people stain the same and it showed since he had put his on thicker. However Dave looked at it and he said we could use the hand sander and put it right, but it did not work. I did not like the colour of the mahogany stain since there was too much red in it. The next day I bought a dark oak stain and went over it.

When the work for the day was finished, I popped into Ploërmel for some milk. On the way back, the lake was smothered with sea birds, obviously after a quick bite to eat perhaps a shoal of fish. I have never seen so many birds on the lake before or since.

I had to go then to the pharmacie with Les because he had been sawing timber and something had gone into his eye. It was beginning to look very red and swollen and both Joan and I had a good look but could not see anything. Pharmacies over here take a more active role in providing much more of a hands-on service than in the UK. The pharmacist examined the eye thoroughly, but like us he could not see anything, saying he would give Les some drops and if it did not clear he must go and see the eye specialist. Two days later the eye was no better so we went to see the eye specialist. It was like a doctor's surgery in England. At the reception desk we had great difficulty trying to explain what was wrong with Les's eye but they asked us to sit down and after waiting for one hour, it was our turn to go in to see the specialist. The man spoke some English and he gave Les more drops and ointment. He said that if it did not resolve in four days it would mean surgery. Thankfully the treatment worked so surgery was not required.

The following day Les went with the over sized contractor Robert, in his small ancient Citroën to Josselin via the quieter back roads to order and pay for the materials for the fosse septique. After this excursion however, they both required some liquid refreshment and when Les returned he brought a bottle of cassis from Mimi's bar. This had been thoroughly tried and approved in the bar before he purchased the bottle. Cassis is a type of black currant liqueur, which is mixed with dry white wine. We were told to only put a small amount of cassis at the bottom of the glass, because it is very strong.

It certainly improves cheap dry white wine. Les's eye was getting better with Joan's careful daily administration of the drops and ointment.

We had decided to give the plastering work to Lee, who had said he would do one of the walls and if we liked it he would continue or if not - no loss - we would have a wall plastered for free. We liked the wall when he had finished plastering and hopefully, it would all be done by January 2000 for me to decorate. This would be ideal except that we did not know his address and had lost his phone number - after much searching we managed to get his approximate address and found his house eventually to give him the go ahead.

The day we were due to return home, we had decided to leave early and visit Fougeres on the way to Caen. This former stronghold is built in a picturesque setting on a promontory overlooking the winding valley of the Narcon. Below it, on a rocky height almost encircled by the river, stands a magnificent feudal castle whose walls, with their thirteen big towers, are among the most massive in Europe. The town centre was quaint and it had been transformed into a pedestrian precinct. There are classical buildings throughout the area. Fougeres, standing as it does between Brittany and the rest of France acquired great military importance in the Middle Ages, when its Barons were very powerful. Victor Hugo and Balzac in Les Chouans introduced Fougeres and its region into their stories of the royalist rebellion. However we walked round the castle walls and into the gardens since it was a nice day and quite warm. We found a typical French bistro where we had morning coffee and returned later for our lunch of gallettes (pancakes- savoury). I choose ham, the others had pork and onions and mushrooms, washed down with some fruity red wine. I could not imbibe to much because it was my turn to drive to the port. We all enjoyed our visit to Fougeres vowing on our next visit we would go inside the castle but today we were pushed for time although we arrived at the port with time to spare. The forecast for the weather was not good and the crossing was rough with high waves and heavy rain and strong winds. We were thankful to reach Portsmouth.

CHAPTER TWELVE

Plastered at Last

Our next trip to France was early in January 2000 and we left home at 4am in freezing fog. Les thankfully drove as far as Newbury where we stopped for a break at our usual service station and where the driver changes. I drove on to Portsmouth arriving at 7.15am, half an hour before the boat sailed. When we checked in, the man at the kiosk warned us that the French lorry drivers were blockading the French ports. Their lorry drivers wanted a thirty five hour week. All vehicles were being stopped, we were given a leaflet by the man at the check in which said ordinary cars were getting through and it was only the freight traffic that demonstrators were stopping. When we embarked we found the boat almost deserted. This trip we sailed on the Val de Loire, the boat that normally does the Le Havre crossing in the summer months. Les happened to see the Captain in the cafeteria and he said there were only 25 passengers and 16 crew and only 3 freight drivers. We arrived at Caen at 4.45 English time, at one stage during the journey the boat stopped for what seemed ages and we suspected that we were waiting to catch the tide. This boat is very large and when we neared the port we could see many sand banks showing and a boat of this size must draw a lot of water. For the duration of the crossing we went into one of the lounges picking three couches which enabled us to have a sleep. I had packed plenty of sandwiches that kept us going with the usual tea from the Salon de Thé. The day before we had left home I had bought cooked lemon and garlic chicken for the sandwiches and it made a change from beef. With our second meal Les bought a bottle of vin rouge which was an improvement on the tea.

We visited the shops on board, but goods had risen in price considerably following the ending of the duty free system. We bought some chocolate to take with us to the house in France and usual gifts we make to our French neighbours, Yvonne and Hélén.

I noticed that there was a press photographer on board who was intending to take pictures of the three UK lorry drivers at the point of the blockade. He was talking with one of the lorry drivers and they were planning to run the blockade if possible. The journey seemed slow but the sea was calm and for January this was unusual. When we arrived at Caen, there was a considerable number of lorries and lots of police but luckily they had left a narrow space between the lorries for cars. We did not have any trouble getting through although it was by going the wrong way, round at roundabouts.

Les drove and Dave navigated so I made myself comfortable on the back seat for a nap. It was beginning to get dark so we wanted to make some headway. Unfortunately we took a wrong turn off the motorway which delayed us, but however we were short on diesel, so it turned out to be a blessing in disguise. I spotted a sign for fuel so we headed in that direction. Eventually we found the garage that was miles from anywhere and hoped that we could find our way back to the motorway. We filled the tank up and I made a quick cup of coffee from the flask and off we went again. The drive back to the motorway was very difficult but thanks to Dave who is a very good navigator we found it, but our troubles were far from over. In England we had seen on the television, that France had been having very bad gales and as we progressed further south, we noticed that many of the road direction signs had been blown down which did not help when trying to find our way in the dark. Dave had lost the torch when he had got out to spend a penny, so we had to put the light on in the car to see the map, however despite all this - more by luck than judgement our journey eventually progressed. We began to settle down and by this time we were due to change drivers. Dave would drive next, but first we had another drink and a sandwich. As we set off again thinking things were going our way at last, another problem arose.

We had just left Caulnes and a bright light shone at us and we were pulled over by a Gendarme. I thought, "I don't believe it what now- we were certainly not speeding". Les put his window down and politely said "bon soir monsieur" The policeman said "votre papiers s'il vous plait". Les, who does not hear well at the best of times, thought he wanted him to quote the car number, thinking that the police thought we had nicked the car. Its funny, but when sometimes you are nervous, do you ever feel you want to laugh? I started to titter which did not amuse the policemen. I said "Les he wants your papers, driving licence and passports". Eventually Les produced the papers that he gave to the Gendarme who looked at the paper on top, which was the E111, medical expenses reclaim form, seemed to be satisfied and gave them back and waved us on.

We arrived in Quelneuc 8.30pm English time. The first problem we found was we could not open the front door and we found out later that the plasterer who had been working on the house in our absence had broken the key off in the lock. We went round to the back door and fortunately we were able to get in. The first thing we all wanted to see was how many rooms had the plasterer done, because we were desperate to get on with the decorating. Lee had not finished all the rooms as promised and Les was not happy with this. My concern was the mess - plaster everywhere and the mice had been having a ball, but later what I had thought to be mice droppings was grain which had dropped from between the floor boards after the plasterer had been banging. Because the upstairs had been used as a granary and the floor boards being the original, were not tongued and grooved, had shrunk leaving gaps between them.

    Thank goodness I had made a casserole before we left home, so all I needed to do was warm it through. We unpacked the car and

I did a quick clean round the kitchen and I made up the beds and filled the hot water bottles. We had gin and tonics all round and the meal was on the table by 10.30pm. Les said he was going to ring Lee and find out why he had not completed the work. As I went to wash up and all the lights went out but luckily we found the candles which we keep handy as this has happened before. When the candles were lit, Dave sorted the electrics and light was restored. Les arrived back from the beach telephone kiosk, from where he had only succeeded in leaving a message on Lee's answer phone, so he would ring the plasterer again in the morning. We were all shattered and despite the fire we were all cold, so we decided to retire. Les was awake first, having had a troubled night thinking about the plastering, so he made the morning cups of tea. I made breakfast, washed up and then cleaned all the house and then prepared to start staining the floor boards in our bedroom. The floorboards in this part of the house were very old, consequently they were difficult to stain. The wood worms had been ahead of me and despite treatment the boards had retained the scars of where the little worms had been and it was very difficult to stain in the cracks. However, when it was finished, it certainly was an improvement and I felt it had cleaned the boards as well as giving them some colour and added character to the room. Dave was busy securing some of the plasterboards and Les went off to phone Lee, yet again. Later when I had finished the bedroom floor I stained the screen in the entrance hall. This looked very much in-keeping with the new front door. Les arrived back and apparently Lee had got another job on and he would be in to see us at 6pm that evening. That would be a nuisance just at the time we ate our evening meal. I decided to delay the meal until 7pm.

In our absence René had, as we had arranged with him, dug out with his tractor, some of the parking area for the other house - which was another job done.

We all worked hard that day and Lee duly arrived at 7pm not at 6pm as promised - I felt I could not win and our meal had to be kept on hold for another hour.

It was agreed Lee would come back on Thursday with another man and finish plastering the walls. Les was happy with this. After eating dinner, I said I would remain indoors and catch up on a few chores. Les and Dave went to see Mimi since Les had received a letter in the UK from the French planning office, yet again, stating " dossier incomplet" regarding our application for work to be done on the other two houses. We were unable to understand precisely what further information they required. Mimi was very helpful, as usual, in translating these letters, after we had exhausted our knowledge of the French language. We had understood from the letter that they were suggesting that we consult a professional architect, which we did not want to do since Les had prepared the planning documents for the first house without paying an architect. Les's plans had been accepted without any problems. For the other two houses we had supplied the same information, photographs and measurements. However, there had been a new officer for authorising planning approvals and as they say "new brooms sweep clean". Mimi said that the letter, even in French, was unclear and she telephoned the Mairie's office next morning. Mimi made arrangements to accompany Les to a rendez - vous with the head of the planning department on the following day. At this meeting the outstanding points, whatever they were, seemed to be remedied and the meeting seemed to achieve the required result.

The following day was icy cold with a small flurry of snow- none of us could believe it. Apparently it is almost unheard of over here. The high winds had blown the roof tiles off René's barn whilst we had been in England and a large fir tree in their garden had been blown down, clipping the end of the apex of our outbuilding. However the damage seemed to be in keeping with the condition of the rest of the roof. I had noticed, on my walks, that many trees had been uprooted and many buildings had been damaged.

Work was hard and I think we were all feeling the pressure due to the time limit in which we had to complete the work on the house. The aim was to finish the work on this house before Les could take time off to go into hospital for his hip replacement. I now continued staining the landings and the other bedroom floors. Two of these were quite easy because it was new wood. Dave continued with filling holes and making good the plasterboard ready for Lee. I had to go along to the dustbin that day and my fingers were frozen - it was just like being in England. We ate our meal early because Lee would be arriving at 6pm. to tape up the plaster board joints ready for the plastering the following day. He arrived on time and worked until 9pm. None of us felt like going out that night since we were all too tired.

Suzannah, one of our granddaughters, had loaned us her compact disc player and it was lovely to be able to sit back and relax and listen to some decent music. I had brought a selection of my compact discs from home. We went to bed at 11pm but I had a bad night with my cough due to the aftermath of the flu' we all had over Christmas. We were up early ready for Lee and his buddy Colin to arrive. They worked all day solidly - hardly stopping for a drink. I offered them food but it was refused Lee said I am not paying Colin to eat - he is here for work. I just supplied them with drinks and the odd biscuit. They worked hard and the results were impressive. The rooms in the house were at last, beginning to look finished and we were pleased with the results. I continued, yet again, to stain the floors and in the process, I was getting covered in brown stain and the fumes from the stain were getting to me. My next job was to paint the skirting boards which was another kneeling job - my poor knees will never be the same again.

The weather the next day was wet but the temperature had risen thank goodness. Work progressed with our motley crew. There was Lee tall young full of confidence, where as his side kick was a weedy little chap - but I felt sorry for him since he looked as if a good meal would not go a miss. He apparently acted as house mother when he was not helping Lee out. His main job was to prepare the plaster mixes for Lee to put on the walls. At coffee time, I had made some Barra-breidd and I gave them a slice with butter. Lee was complaining about some of the plasterboards that had been put up on the landing ceiling. There was some movement of the plasterboards so they had to come down and be replaced.

René was again asking Les about buying the land behind the house we were selling. Les had hesitated about this because of the sale of the house but eventually decided to let René have it. We noticed that the posts had not been put out far enough but I am pleased to say the surveyor instructed René to move them to where he had driven his boundary pegs in the ground.

The plasterers continued to work hard although they did a lot of arguing, which I found entertaining. Mainly the arguments were concerning the state of the plaster mix that was either too wet or too dry. By now I had christened the little one half-pint. Whilst we worked, Dave insisted having Pavarotti punching out in the background. At one stage, Lee asked if we could have another disc on for a bit of light relief and I obliged much to the dismay of Dave. Later that day, Yvonne arrived with a plate full of crêpes that were delicious having cooked them with some sort of lemon sauce. They were all eaten in a matter of minutes. Lee finished his plastering and Les settled up with him. Dave and I went for a walk to Ville Armel and then back by the lake.

Hélén, our neighbour, was not well after her operation. I bought her some chocolate that I took to her house but could not see anyone so I decided to call back later.

The next day, Dave finished boxing in the pipes in the kitchen and when this was done he removed one or two rotten floor boards from the lounge and replaced them with new wood and put skirting board around the salon which looked much better. Skirting board is not usually seen on this type of house but we thought that they would make life more difficult for any mouse to gain admission. By now I had finished staining all the bedrooms leaving just the landing and stairs to do.

The next day, Les suggested we invite Mimi out for a meal, as a way of thanking her for her successful help with the planning authorities. That evening we went up to see Mimi at the bar. We asked her if she would like to come out with us for a meal one evening, but she said in evenings, she was always working and she was very busy at the moment rehearsing her part in the local play. We were disappointed but decided we would go out ourselves since we had all been working hard and deserved a treat. Les booked to go for a meal to Le Saigon - a Thai restaurant. The restaurant was orientally decorated and the staff was very friendly and not very busy with only another three couples apart from us. We thoroughly enjoyed our meals since the food was very good. I had chosen a prawn starter with salads and the men both had soup. I had duck for my main course, one of the men had pork and the other one beef. Sweets were delicious. I had banana fritters, Dave had similar but with cognac and Les had lychees. The wine was very good and so was the Chinese beer, which was new to the men, but gained their seal of approval. After our meal we were given, with compliments of the house, some saki, which is rice, based spirit, to drink that was very strong. The cups, in which the sakis were served, were small and made of very fine bone china. When we each drained our cup

there was a picture on the bottom. Mine was a picture of a male stripped off and when the men came to the bottom of their cups - guess what - a picture of a woman stripped off. We all had a good laugh. Dave and I ate our meals with chopsticks but Les used a fork.
" With the use of chop sticks" Les said to me" it certainly slows you down - so you should use these for all meals" It is a running joke in the family that I always finish my food first, followed a close second by Suzannah, one of our granddaughters. Les said " one of these times you will succeed in finishing your meal before our guests have started". We bid our farewells to the waiter and said we would be returning when we came on another visit to France. The waiter said we could keep the chopsticks and Dave made a little stand for them so they now hold pride of place on the kitchen windowsill.

The next day we decided we would need to stay longer in order to finish the work, so Les changed the boat booking to the weekend. My next job was to lay the floor tiles in the shower room. They were made of vinyl and were very difficult to stick down, but when finished they did look effective, but I would not use the same type again. That evening we went for a ride round to Loyat and St Malo 3 Fountaines but all the bars were closed as it was wintertime and it is difficult to find anywhere open in the evenings.

The following day Bertrand visited us to take on the agency for the sale of the property. We agreed on the sale price and arrangements were made for the property to go on the market. We had also arranged in England for the property to be placed on the French Property News website for private sales and we would then pass any enquiries to Bertrand for viewing arrangements. We intended also to have 300 brochures of the house on display at their French property exhibition to be held in Birmingham in March 2000.

That evening we went to the bar in Ploërmel and the men played pool but unfortunately a chap there had been drinking a lot and he became a bother such as asking us for money and passing some unfortunate remarks, so we decided not to stay.

The next day they put two more collars under the inspection lid of the new septic tank to raise its level. It was necessary for the new septic tank installation, to be above the expected lawn level.

I put up curtains to all of the windows and stained the landing floor. After which I went to the local garden centre to buy some silk flowers. Les had made a hard wood polished plinth at the top of the stairs beneath the window and it was just crying out for a vase of flowers. The vase and flowers looked attractive against the window as you walked up the stairs and I began to wish we were not selling this house.

The next day it was better weather so Dave and I went for a brief walk, taking the usual path by the lake but on this day after so much rain the ground underfoot was extremely wet and muddy. Needless to say my shoes were ruined but they were already passed their best. During our walk we were looking at the land we had sold to René and at the bottom of the field was a small building. Being nosey, Dave went to take a look and thank goodness I did not follow because the cows electric fence had fallen down and Dave did not see it, trod on it and had an electrical shock - described by him as a real belt. That may teach him not to be so inquisitive.

In the afternoon I cleaned the lounge floor with wood cleaner and applied lots of floor wax which I rubbed into the floor boards- it was very hard work. In the meantime Dave went into the next house and found some spare wood and proceeded to make an old fashioned bumper with which to polish the floor. This took me back a few years to when I had just started nursing and the ward maids used to polish the ward floors like this. The bumper was very heavy because Dave had found two large rocks that he placed on the top of it to give more weight and a better resultant shine. As luck would have it this made the bumper much too heavy for me to use. Dave volunteered and I must say he did a sterling job when he had finished the floor shone like glass. Alfred came round and invited us for drinks so I was able to give Hélén her chocolate. David trimmed the front door and put the weatherboard on it. We noticed from our letterbox contents that we were now on the mailing list for promotions from the local supermarkets. This may save us a few francs.

We were due to return home so we rose early, had a rushed breakfast, packed the car and my last job was to stain the stairs before leaving. In the meantime Yvonne arrived to sit with us at breakfast. We were ready to leave at 9.30. We decided that we would go to Bayeux for Dave to see the Tapestry. Unfortunately when we got there the building was closed for refurbishing, so we decided to go to some of the beaches used in the Normandy D-Day landings. What a journey this turned out to be since we had miscalculated on the time and after leaving the beaches we needed to step on it in order to catch the ferry. We were the last car to arrive at the port with two minutes to spare and an escort by the ferry patrol van, but we made it - by the skin of our teeth.

CHAPTER THIRTEEN

Twinkle Toes and Tequila

On the next visit, someone had said we should try to find Mûr-de – Bretagne. I had also read in a book that this town was one of Brittany's most popular inland resorts and nearby is the lake Lac de Guerlédan which was formed by a dam built on the Blavet river in the 1920's. Nearby was the Daoulas gorge, which is reputed to be a spectacular feature. Having eventually located this, we were not particularly impressed. When we started our journey, the sun was still hot for early evening. We had travelled about 65 miles when we came in sight of the lake. It had been easy to find glittering in the evening sunlight and the scenery was beautiful. The tourist guide had named the area La Suisse Brettonne and we could readily see the reason for this comparison.

Not far away from the lake was a well-tended ruin of a Cistercian abbey - not unlike our English Tintern Abbey.

Beside this abbey was a large hotel called Bon Repos, which was a most impressive building and appeared to be built in the same stonework as the abbey. We were told by one of the staff there, that the hotel had been renovated in 1982.

Les suggested after we had finished looking around the lakeside, that we have a drink at the hotel. We readily agreed, as we were eager to see the inside of the hotel.

The entrance was most impressive as we entered the courtyard under a large stone archway. We crossed the lawn by stepping on stones laid there, I suspect to avoid damage caused by heavy shoes and high heels on the beautiful lawn. When we walked into the reception area, we were asked if we wished to eat and we explained that we had already eaten but would like to have a drink. We were shown into a large room with a bar at the far end. The walls of the room were in exposed patterned stonework, looking most impressive. There were large paintings of Breton landscapes hanging on the walls and there were several small tables with chairs dotted around the room, on a well-polished wooden floor. On our way in, we had passed through the dining area where two vociferous french families were eating but there was no one in the bar except us. Shortly, a rather strange looking man entered the room and positioned himself behind the bar. His greeting was friendly and he asked us what we would like to drink. Les had a whisky liqueur, David a beer and Joan and I had brandy. I could not take my eyes off the man who was wearing what I believed to be a black boater type hat – probably Breton in origin. His skin was sallow with a look of parchment about it. His trousers were black and he wore a brightly coloured waistcoat over his white shirt and he and his attire, fitted in completely with the surroundings. When he had served us with our drinks he departed, to reappear with a dish full of sugar lumps, giving Joan and I a demonstration of how we were to place the sugars lumps in our mouths and sip the brandy through them. He departed yet again, reappearing this time with some dark chocolates for us. In a far corner of the room, I had noticed a keyboard a guitar and some other musical instruments and whilst I was looking at them, our friend "the hat", sat down and began to play the keyboard. He was an accomplished musician and it was most enjoyable sitting there in such lovely surroundings, letting the music drift over you. He suggested that we should grace his playing by taking to the dance floor. David asked Joan for a dance but she declined, so he asked me. I was a little shy at first, since we were the only couple dancing, but I soon got over it and we danced between the tables to Frank Sinatra song `I did it my way'. Les said to `the hat' pointing laughingly "Frank Sinatra." He replied in broken English "No - I am much younger" and laughed." He was pleased we recognised the tune, and went on to play Strangers in the Night. Les got up and danced which was amazing because he was still recovering from his hip replacement. We ordered a second round of drinks and our little Frenchman had a drink of coke with us, after which he returned to the keyboard and sang a few more numbers for us, in his soothing voice. We bought some postcards of pictures of the hotel and local scenes, to remind us of our special evening out. Before we left we were given cards telling us about the hotel .In the reception area we looked at the menu and not surprisingly the cost for a meal was about £26 per head. In all it was a most enjoyable evening and we were pleased to have made a friend of our little musician. We promised to return for a meal when we came to France the next time.

During the evening, Les said "my wife plays the organ" and I was promptly asked if I would like to play but enough was enough for one evening, the fact I had danced was an achievement in its self, after so many years. When we left we went for a drive round part of the lake and we stopped briefly to take a photograph, but soon returned to the car when it began to rain. David drove back to Quelneuc. We had really enjoyed the evening. David called me twinkle toes, but qualified this by saying that I had been very stiff when I first got up to dance, but soon relaxed when I got into the rhythm.

The following evening we went for a drink at Mimi's. The bar was very busy on this evening because it was Ascension day the following day and everyone would be on holiday .We remained with her longer than usual, because there were a couple of troublesome youngsters, who had drunk too much. Mimi asked Les and David if we would wait until they departed. We readily agreed to stay and Mimi introduced us to Tequila sunrise, which was potent and refreshing, but I would not be making a habit of drinking it for my head the next morning felt as if a donkey had kicked me. During the evening we had been talking about security, with Mimi being on her own. She explained that because she was a woman normally she had no trouble from the men since they usually would do as she asked. If it had been a man telling them to leave they may be difficult. She explained to us how she had hung round the walls several mirrored adverts. She could be sat anywhere in the bar and could see what was happening, even when she had her back to customers. By looking through the mirrors, she was able too observe what everyone was doing. Mimi owned two very large black dogs (father and son), that were very protective of her. She made the point she could not let the dogs become involved, if there was any trouble, because if they were to bite anyone, they would have to be put down. Eventually we bid our farewells at nearly midnight when the two boys had gone, fortunately without making any trouble.

After we had got home, I had just put on the kettle to make a drink when there was a knock on the door. A little voice saying "Jill nanny" was heard. That could only be one person - my grandson, Ben. Whatever could they be doing here at this time of night. I opened the door and in walked my son, Richard, his partner and their son. They were on their way to see the Grand Prix at Monaco. I quickly made up two beds, fed and watered them and we all went to bed - that is except for Les and Richard because Richard wanted Les to do a route to the south of France for him.

Richard was very complimentary about the house and the surrounding area. He said that he was surprised at the size of the house and he thought the oak beams and the old fireplace, were lovely.

The next morning we had our breakfast at the normal time for us. The visitors slept on until 10am. They looked much better for a good sleep. Ben was chirpy as usual and they ate an English cooked breakfast. They had planned to have a two week holiday under canvas but knowing how disorganised my son's family is, I dreaded to think what sort of holiday they would be having.

For example they had not yet bought any sleeping bags. They had planned to buy them that day in France but they had not realised that it was Ascension Day and all shops would be closed. To top it all, they were low on fuel for the car but luckily René, the farmer knew a garage owner who would sell them some fuel, but they had to drive miles out into the country to get it. After this it was midday, so they all stayed for lunch. After lunch we all walked down to the lake and then after a cup of tea, they finally set off. I am quite sure if I had said stay for another day, they would have been pleased to do so but when my family are around no work gets done. They finally went with food and a big blanket to sleep under until they could get the sleeping bags.

Early that evening, Les and Dave went to Mimi's bar and they were a little late coming back. The meal I had prepared was getting cold so I decided enough was enough and locked the doors and pretended to be out, leaving a note on the door saying 'restaurant closed.' After a while, we heard them muttering outside. Dave said "Les haven't you got a key" "No" he replied "Jill has it". After a short while we heard footsteps upstairs. Dave had only scaled the wall and climbed in through an open upstairs window. When we had recovered from the fright of hearing someone upstairs, we re-opened the restaurant.

On Friday, Les bought some paint for me to paint the outside windows and doors downstairs of Pré du Lac to keep me out of mischief. Our aim was to get the outside of the property looking as good as the inside, if possible.

I had made a good friend of Rudi, the farm puppy, so good that he ran off with my T-shirt which had been airing on the clotheshorse. Rudi, unlike his predecessor Belle, was wild and rather undisciplined.

René was patiently training him to bring the cows in for milking. One day whilst watching them working together, Rudi was scampering after the young cows, barking at their heels to keep them moving. However there was one old cow, obviously a high volume milk producer who refused to take any notice of Rudi and when the dog tried to make her hurry, she lowered her head and bellowed at him. In response he shot of down the field, much to René's annoyance.

The next day was Saturday and the morning was spent finishing all the odd jobs. Yvonne asked me if I was going shopping to Leclerc and if could she come with me. I was delighted she had asked me because it meant we were at last communicating on a reasonable level. We drove to the supermarket, put our 10-Franc coins in our respective trolleys and chatted in French when we crossed paths in the aisles. I felt really pleased with myself and I was interested to see what her weekly shopping consisted of. I noticed that she purchased a large amount of meat. Perhaps she needed this because she catered for René as well as herself.

In the afternoon we went to a local horse show at La Touche which is on the opposite side of the lake from were our house was. It turned out to be very good with some fine horses taking part. I was particularly interested as I had done a lot of riding in my youth and I know David had ridden in the past and thought he would enjoy seeing the horse jumping.

That evening we invited Yvonne, Hélén and Alfred for drinks and snacks. This event was becoming a customary practice on the evening before our departure. We were beginning to chat easily with one another, but still not without the odd mime or two to help with the communications. Eventually we bid our farewells and said we would be off early but would see them in July. Before we retired to bed, as is now our custom before going away we have a look at the lake. Joan and I were walking ahead and when we reached the waters edge, I spotted a movement and a little head appeared above the water. I realised that it was an otter, accompanied by another little one. They kept diving and popping up further out from the bank but sadly by the time the men arrived they had disappeared.

When the day of departure arrived, the sun was shining. Dave bought our tea at 5.30 and we were up for 6am, with breakfast completed we departed at 7am.

Yvonne bid us farewell and we made St Malo in good time the sea was like a millpond. Another successful trip concluded!

CHAPTER FOURTEEN

Suzannah and Emma

Our next ferry crossing was smooth with hardly a ripple on the sea. This time Les, David and I were accompanied by two of our grandchildren, Emma and Suzannah.

Because the sea was so calm, Suzannah who was not a good traveller did not require the bowl on this occasion. From when she was very small, we always carried a bowl in the car.

The children had been to France once before with us but that had been several years ago with their mother Ruth and cousins Rachel and Tracey. On this occasion we rented a gîte in Dieppe to go to Euro Disney in Paris. Finding the location of the latter was more difficult than we expected. Eventually we stopped at a bar to enquire the way and by sheer coincidence there was a girl who worked there, who suggested that we followed her car. The sign posting from the centre of Paris had confused us, because it had shown Vallée de Marne rather than Disney World. We returned to Paris by midnight and were offered a car wash between the legs of the Eiffel Tower, which we accepted.

Emma was now 12 years old and could not remember much about the previous trip - only that she had visited Disney World. Susannah who was now 15 years old could remember a little more.

The boat on which we sailed for Caen, was the Duc de Normandy which is the one on which I am usually sick, but this time no one felt in the least queasy. We sat for most of the six hours on the deck, sunbathing. I had packed a picnic lunch before leaving home, so we were able to enjoy this outside on the deck .The girls liked the boat crossing and spent much of the journey exploring the boat facilities including shops, gaming machines, practising their French language skills on the crew and sunbathing.

The drive from Caen to Quelneuc was better than previous visits with more of the new motorways and we did not meet the ROUTE BARRE sign once. When we arrived at the house, my first action is always to check what cleaning is necessary. I must admit it was very good this time with even the fridge still open and spotless. As we approached the beginning of our lane, René observed our arrival from his tractor and when he saw us, his face lit up into a large grin and he waved to us as we passed by. He was working late bringing in the harvest and making the most of the light evenings. The girls were very excited at the prospect of their holiday, looking all over the house and scampering in and out of the rooms. I told them they could choose their bedroom and they picked the one Joan usually sleeps in, overlooking the farm .I didn't tell them that the cows are first milked at some unearthly hour in the morning and the milking machine may awaken them.

Once the beds were made up I started cooking the evening meal which consisted of pork and apple burgers, sausages, bacon, eggs and tomatoes. All very fattening but everyone loved it. After our meal we went to visit Mimi and we introduced her to the girls who were amazed at how well she spoke English. I didn't tell them that she was the only French person they would hear speaking English in Quelneuc. The evening was enjoyable and the girls thought it was wonderful being allowed up so late. They amused themselves playing on the football machine, while the three adults caught up on the village gossip with Mimi.

We went to bed about midnight, shattered. The following morning David was up as usual at the crack of dawn having made our first cup of tea. We had decided to leave the girls to sleep in. We were able to get breakfast and wash up before Emma surfaced and

Susannah was not far behind. They didn't want breakfast except for just a drink, so we decided to go to the shops to buy some milk and fresh French bread. I had given them both some pocket money and knowing them it would not be very long before it was all spent. On the way to the shops we drove by the lakeside and the girls could not believe their eyes. Emma exclaimed "isn't it big" and Suzannah wanted to know which part of the lake they could swim in. I promised to take them down to the lake to show them after lunch.

That afternoon I went swimming with them since the weather was glorious and the sun was very hot. The water was warm and although I had not been looking forward to swimming in a lake, as I preferred the sea because I had visions of murky water and lots of weed in the lake, but I was wrong. The four hundred yards of man-made beach had fine, clean sand. The swimming area was separated from the rest of the lake by marker buoys to keep boats out. There were facilities for buying drinks and ice cream by the beach. I put on my swimming costume and followed the girls into the water. We all enjoyed ourselves swimming and sun bathing for the afternoon.

The girls had brought two airbeds with them and Emma insisted that I got on one of them in the water. This I found was not an easy feat and by the time I had fallen off twice, much to Emma's delight, I said that enough was enough and I was going to lie on the beach to have a snooze. We all put on sun protection cream but both girls got very red but by the end of the holiday they went home nice and brown.

That evening, after dinner we invited our new Irish neighbours who lived opposite, to come round for a drink. They had, like us, bought an old house for renovation. A very quiet German chap had done the renovation of their house. We told them that we had tried in the past, to get into conversation with him, but he would not respond. They laughed at this replying that Harold had a thing about the English. In his opinion, they were not like the Irish. He thought the English were only in France because they could not make a go of it in their own country. Our neighbours were friendly and amusing company. Michael was an electronics engineer with an aircraft company, his wife Barbara worked in a school three days a week and they had one ten-year-old son, Carl. Their home was in Belfast. The evening seemed to go quickly with a few bottles of wine consumed and much interesting conversation.

The following day I took the girls to the beach and arranged to pick them up at 4 o'clock. On this visit, I was determined to wash the loose covers from the settees and arm chairs because foolishly, I believed that all the dirty work in the house was finished. I had not realised what work David would be doing. However at this point in time I was not to know so I went ahead and washed them. They soon dried in the sun and I had to dampen them down to iron them. They looked really clean when I had finished, with the colours reappearing as new.

One of the jobs for the men was to dig out the ditch at the front of the house to investigate the problem of static water building up and smelling, near to the front door. The problem was found to be that the road and roof drainage was not piped away at this point. This necessitated laying pipes on a concrete base after which David concreted round the sides of them and cut slots along the length of the pipes to take roof water away since there is no guttering at this point. We proceeded to make a concrete manhole to receive water from three pipes found, of somewhat doubtful source. David inscribed his name as the creator of the manhole for the benefit of and to confuse future archaeologists. We then placed gravel over the pipes on top of which we placed flower tubs and filled them with geraniums, micklemas daisies and fuchsias.

Michael and Barbara very kindly offered the use of their bicycles to the two girls. They soon took up this offer. The area around Quelneuc is very quiet and so long as they remembered to ride on the right hand side of the road they would be fine. Emma persuaded me to go for a bike ride although I had not ridden a bike for years and after the ride my legs ached from the use of muscles I didn't know I had.

The following day was Saturday and Josselin always has a market and the town is only about 8 miles away. I thought the girls would like to see it to give them the opportunity to look for gifts to take back home. The morning was warm and sunny when we left home soon after nine. When we arrived in Josselin, we found parking quite difficult with so many people already there. The girls soon found plenty of things to interest them. Emma bought some wind chimes to take home for her mother and Suzannah bought a rattle for her little brother. I bought a sweatshirt for Emma, with dolphins on it, which she said she would like. I did some shopping for vegetables and then we returned home for lunch. In the afternoon, I left the girls at the lake, which gave me a chance to do some painting by the front door. That evening there was a summer fete in Ploërmel, which consisted of several stalls selling all types of drinks, and you could also buy bags of pomme frites which both the girls had. There was a group playing Breton music, in traditional costume. All age groups were dancing, so when Emma insisted I got up with her to dance, I did. After a while we got the hang of the dance steps and away we went. The dancing was held in the main square in front of the hôtel de ville. It was followed by a fire work display, which did not start until 12 midnight. It was well worth waiting for, with an excellent display of fireworks accompanied by appropriate music. The setting was very impressive in front of the old chateau type building of the hôtel de ville (the name for the mayor's house or place of work). It added atmosphere, the music ranged from Beatles to Beethoven

The next day was Sunday and I wanted the girls to come with me to Mass at the village church. I thought that they would find the service a little different to the way it was in England. How appropriate this proved to be. In the villages around Quelneuc during the summer months, each of the little churches, take it in turn to hold Mass. This week it was to be held at the church of St Anne at Lezilliac and of course it was held outside as the church was to small to hold the entire congregation. It was a lovely sunny morning and when we arrived in plenty of time, many people were already there. We sat on some little benches in front of a portable altar. A keyboard with microphone had been set up so we could hear the priests say Mass and have an accompaniment for the hymns. The two priests welcomed everyone and afterwards we were invited to have a drink of wine or soft drink and something to eat. We met Peter and Edith. They also were on holiday with their children. We promised to meet up with them at a later date.

In the afternoon we visited a Battages fête which is an exhibition which includes old tractors, bailers, threshing machines, donkey engines and much more machinery used by the farmers over the years. On the same site, was a beautiful old manor house that was currently being restored. Not far from the house was a very old, fascinating, high round building, in good state of repair, made of natural stone. There were specially formed gaps in the stonework and we realised this was a dovecote. This building was now used for displaying local paintings and craftwork. At the fête there were stalls for buying food and drinks. Near to the dovecote there was an ancient bread oven. The farmer's wife had prepared some dough and we were shown how it was made and shaped into a round loaf, then olive oil was brushed lightly over the loaves before they were placed in the bread oven. The oven was a large stone built mound which was hollow inside with a chimney through which smoke was pouring so obviously there was a good fire going underneath. Earth and grass to avoid heat loss covered the oven. After the bread had been placed into the oven, it was an hour before it was cooked. We purchased two loaves, which we had ordered to be made in this oven, to take home. That evening we ate one of the loaves with French butter and Brie cheese and it was delicious.

The countryside where the fête was held really was quite beautiful, with contrasting colours of the green maize fields with the golden cornfields. It was a picture to behold and dotted over the countryside were small Breton houses, lived in by the farming community. Many of the ladies were dressed in the Breton tradition of black dress with white lace head-dress. Several of the old farmers were busy tying to get a donkey engine started with the help of one of the tractors, but belts kept slipping. David was simply itching to go and help them but was restrained from doing so since we could not steal their thunder. Eventually they got it going and with this engine they were able to start the threshing mill. We watched this for some time, the girls finding it very interesting, seeing how the seeds were separated from the wheat sheaves.

During the afternoon a group of Breton musicians arrived and entertained the onlookers with their music, which I must admit I am sold on. Emma was also enthused by the music and our feet were itching to dance. Later that day there was to be a pig roast, followed by dancing but unfortunately it began to rain which was not a gentle downpour but a real torrential storm. When it started I had taken the children to look for a toilet which unfortunately we could not find, so we had to go behind a hedge. Emma the little monkey shouted "watch out granny someone is coming" I jumped up quick nearly causing myself an injury and she shouted that she was only joking. Grannie was not amused! In the meantime the men were sheltering in the dovecote but we were drenched so we thought it best to get home and into some dry clothing.

The next day David finished doing the manhole outside the front of Pre du Lac. Les and Emma had put down some ornamental edging stones and with the pots full of flowers, it looked very much better. Unfortunately we were not allowed to put up the costly chain link fence which we bought in a garden centre in England. René came over when we had just put in the second post saying that planning permission would be required for fencing. He did not think we would get it because the land right up to the wall of the houses did not belong to the owner of the houses. We were disappointed but we did not wish to be involved in a planning dispute at this stage particularly whilst our application was being considered for the alterations we were to make to the other houses.

On the Wednesday Hélén, our friend and neighbour came round and invited us to her house for drinks, just before lunch. When we arrived there we found that René and Alfred were already there. The girls drank coke and I had what I believe to be a port, which I enjoyed but was not ideal when you are working all afternoon. The men drank beer and shortly after our arrival two other men arrived, to whom we were introduced and very soon everyone was chatting away in French. One of the men whose name escapes me, spoke very slowly which enabled me to understand most of what he said, which was refreshing. It was an enjoyable social interlude. In the afternoon, I was busy doing the chores and the girls had gone out on the bikes. Later that day René took the girls with him to bring in the cows for milking .I laughed to myself because at home Suzannah would run a mile if she saw a cow and here she was bringing in a herd from the field. They watched them being milked and when they returned they bought with them two litres of fresh milk. René had made their visit interesting by explaining to them, how the milk had to be prepared before it is bought from the supermarket. He explained that the milk had to be a certain temperature. The temperature must drop by 5 degrees in the cooler, if it was not, the collecting wagon would not take it and if this happened René would not receive any subsidy.

That evening I heard Emma scream "quick Granny, come quick". When I reached her, I could immediately see the problem since attached to one of the beams, was the biggest dragonfly I had ever seen. I could easily have screamed myself because I dislike them. This goes back a long way to when I was about 6 years old and one of these flies perched on the collar of my coat. I can remember the look on my mother's face when she tried to push it away. This time I quickly called Dave who used the tea towel to cover the fly and then took the thing outside.

After dinner the girls asked if they could go for a walk which was perhaps to get out of washing up. I let them go but within 5 minutes they were back. They said they had spotted a cow by the lake and would we go and see. David and I went to look but when we reached the lake there was no cow to be seen.

The next day we took the girls to see the Forêt de Brocéliande, which as legend has it, was where King Arthur lived. The forest is very dense and beautiful and a joy to visit. On the way, we visited the Château de Trécesson. This is surrounded by very deep and wide moat. Parts of the chateau date back to the end of the fourteenth century, in reddish stone. It still has its medieval appearance with a high gatehouse supported by corbelled turrets creating an impressive entrance. There are many tales around its history such as the one about a bride on her wedding day. The girl had been buried alive near the chateau. A peasant saw the burial and summoned help. Unfortunately by the time the she was dug up she was dead. The girls thought that this was a wonderful story about this spooky place. After leaving the chateau, we reached the market town of Paimpont, (end of the bridge) deep in the forest. We decided to take a walk by the lake. It was a balmy evening and the fish where jumping, so we sat down to watch them. Some time later we found a welcoming Bistro with a garden set out with tables and chairs with a barbecue in full swing but since we had already eaten, we just went in for a drink. We sat outside, the men ordered beer the girls coke and I decided to have a red wine. What I didn't know was, they only sold it by the carafe and when it arrived I said to the men "you will have to help me out with this if I am to drive back".

When it was time to go I started the engine, busily watching a man on the left-hand side of the car and I did not look to the right low down. Unfortunately, I had not seen the four menu boards standing by the roadside. I reversed the car and sent all the boards flying along the road whereupon the girls roared with laughter and of course this started to make me giggle and I could do nothing for laughing. They kept saying that Gran must be tiddly. David was a bit concerned that someone would come out and find all the boards knocked over, so he jumped out of the car and replaced them all neatly as they were before, although he was also helpless with laughter. When the boards were upright once more, I proceeded to reverse instead of driving forward, knocking them down again. It was just too much so I made a quick get away.

That evening we heard that the French Concorde had crashed which soon sobered us up. The following day Mike and Barbara invited us to a barbecue on their new patio. The evening was sunny and the temperature was just right ideal for eating outside. When we arrived at their house we were asked what we would like to drink. I think we all said wine and we sat out on the patio and drank it, enjoying the quiet relaxation of the company and the setting sun. Barbara asked us if we would like to look round their house and we immediately said "yes please" because it is interesting to see how other people have gone about their renovation work. It was a large building with rooms on differing floor levels. I remarked on the floor in the kitchen, which was most attractive with the concrete having been covered with some sort of polyurethane on which Barbara had painted a design. The walls had been plastered but not smooth like ours since theirs was plastered straight on to the stonewalls, which we have many times called character addition. If we fail to make a perfect finish, we now call this adding character. Barbara had a good eye for colour and use of lighting, making the house look light and spacious. In the lounge area they had two french doors leading outside to the rear patio. This would give access to a secluded garden which, was in the process of being created. Mike was busy cooking something that certainly smelt good. The inside of their house was developed completely different to ours, which is the beauty of individual renovations which, allow for different tastes and styles. David commented afterwards that he preferred ours and we told him that he was just biased.

The food was tasty and we complimented Michael on his cooking skills. He had prepared pork chops, savoury sausages, beef burgers, different kinds of salads, rice, new bread and a good selection of french wine. After the meal, the children departed inside to play games and the adults remained outside enjoying the warm evening, exchanging stories of our individual experiences. It was soon midnight and Dave was the first to depart "got to be up early tomorrow" he said. Half an hour later, we said our farewells. We thanked them for a really enjoyable evening.

The following day was a disaster. I mentioned earlier that I had washed all my loose covers and cleaned the house thoroughly ready for the friends who where coming to stay in the house when we returned home. I had said in the past that I thought the fireplace needed a face-lift, but by now I had given up on the idea, because Les had said it looked in character. However, David had been of the same opinion as me and at the first opportunity he had, he decided he would start work on the chimney-breast. Les had gone into Ploërmel and would not be back for some time. I was hanging washing out on the line, when I heard knocking sounds and then something falling on the floor. I went into the lounge to investigate, where I couldn't believe my eyes. My lovely clean room was a shambles with dust everywhere. At least Dave had put a dustsheet on the floor were he was knocking off the old plaster. He had also attempted to cover the chairs near the fireplace, with mats off the floor. Oh men they really are quite impossible. I kept quiet but inwardly I was seething as he carried on chipping the old plaster off the chimney- breast, down to the stonework. As the old stonework started to appear, so my temper began to recede since it really was beginning to look so much better. He continued to mix some sand and cement and after raking out the stone joints, he pointed up with the new mortar. When he had finished, I was glad that I had kept quiet, even though the cleaning had to be done all over again which took me all the rest of that day and the next. I had to re-wax the floor, but David did volunteer to polish it for me, thank goodness.

I went into Medriniac the next day and bought some lovely mats for the bedrooms and a large mat for the lounge. The house was beginning to look like it was cared for.

Our stay was coming to an end the night before we departed we invited Yvonne and Hélén and their families for a drink and a bite to eat. We had also invited our Irish friends from opposite, but unfortunately Barbara had lost one of the passports and they were busy searching for it, so we didn't see them again because they were leaving that evening. I did receive a letter from them when we got back to the U.K. telling me that Barbara had found the passport in her son's Lego box. Perhaps it was their son's way of trying to extend their stay.

We left Quelneuc early on the Sunday morning, with the intention of spending some of the day in Dinan, having lunch there and then making our way to Caen and the boat which left at 4.30 p.m. When we arrived at Dinan, we wandered round the town finding most interesting features. In the old streets, there were many quaint old buildings with sagging timbers and portico architecture. There were many little squares and in one of them a small crowd had gathered to listen to a musician play what looked like a mandolin. He was very good and a joy to listen to. The whole town had a medieval atmosphere about it you could feel as you wondered from street to street. I could imagine meeting characters from the Dickens novel a Tale of two Cities round one of the corners, with a crowd of revolutionaries. Many of the old houses had been beautifully restored making it a most interesting place and we vowed to return when we have more time.

We lunched at a small restaurant in one of the squares, where the service and the food were excellent and the ambience goes without saying. Les choose a medieval salad with ham, I choose a ham galette, and the children had steak and pomme frites and David had mussels that looked very good. For sweet, we all had different ice cream concoctions.

Sadly we had to leave Dinan and make our journey back to catch the boat at Caen. The crossing was good and the children loved wandering all over the boat for most of the journey. David and me busied ourselves with the crosswords and Les went for a walk and then he read for a bit .We ate our picnic and when we had finished it was time to get ready to disembark. It had been a good trip with lots of jobs done and it had also been a good holiday for the girls.

CHAPTER FIFTEEN

Call a Halt and Sell

After we returned home this time we decided that work on the house in France was finished. Our next priority was to sell this house. With Pré du Lac sold we would use the money to renovate the other two houses and the cave, which we planned to keep for our own use.

We wanted to visit the French Property News exhibition held at the Edgbaston cricket ground in Birmingham. This was to confirm that our 300 for sale leaflets explaining about the property and a photograph of the house were prominently displayed at the exhibition. Two weeks later after the advert went on the Internet we had a phone call from a gentleman living in Margate who was very interested in looking at the house, so arrangements were made for him to meet Bertrand over in France. We helped arrange his hotel accommodation and Bertrand would pick him up from the lakeside hotel. The following week Les, David and myself went to the exhibition at which our leaflets were certainly popular. Les insisted that the exhibition organiser's manager placed a large picture of the lake beside the particulars of the house. This would give potential customers an idea of the surrounding area. The calls from people who had seen the property advertised on the Internet kept coming. We were busy making contact with our French estate agent for them to show the potential customers round our property. This was not without its difficulties. A prospective buyer rang us one Friday saying he was playing golf in Lorient the following week and would like to visit our property on the Saturday. He had been in contact with the English person at the estate agent in France and was told he could not show him round the house on that day, saying that he was busy with other people's properties. We were very disappointed about this so I came up with the idea if Bertrand could leave the key with our next door neighbour, our gentleman could collect the key himself and see inside the property. Les rang Bertrand and he agreed to take the key to Yvonne, whilst we waited in anticipation, hoping someone out there will buy Pré du Lac.

We kept in regular contact with our agents in France. There was much interest in the property, from our internet entry, but no one had made an offer for it as yet. Les decided to contact the two potential customers, who had not come back to us, being eager for their comments, and to ask the key question why they were not interested after viewing the house. One of them had settled for another property in Medriniac to be near their friends. He liked our house but the bedrooms in the one he had decided to buy were larger. The second gentleman said it was not for him, much too near a working farm.

We were due to return to Quelneuc in May and no offer had been made although we had over a dozen enquiries. On this trip we were taking Joan and David. On our previous visit Les had discussed the electrics and plumbing for the other house, with Frederick and his father, for our next project. They agreed to do the work on this next house before we returned ready for us to move in furniture, when we sell Pré du Lac.

There were many more enquiries from the Internet, with several people viewing the house whilst we were there. We were keeping our fingers crossed hoping that someone out there would like our house sufficiently to put in an offer.

In the meantime we would start the renovation work on one of the other houses. We decided to leave the middle house until last because it would require more work than the house at the other end of the row. I decided to call this house Travail d'amour (Labour of Love) – it must be this if we were prepared to do the renovation project all over again.

CHAPTER SIXTEEN

The Mouse Returns

The purpose of this visit was to be in Quelneuc when potential buyers came to view Pré du Lac. We took David with us to commence work on Travail d'amour and Joan had come to keep me company and help get Pré du Lac ship shape for any potential buyers. When we arrived in Quelneuc our first job was to switch on the electricity and turn on the water in Pré du Lac, after which the men went to assess the programme of work to be achieved on this visit on the next house we had decided to tackle. Joan was busy removing the plastic sheeting from the chairs and settee when she called me. "Jill come look at this" she said. I went into the lounge and in the middle of the one armchair was a large hole in one of the loose covers. It was too large to sew up so it would mean replacing the cover and I doubt if I would find any material to match as these chairs were about six years old, therefore a throw would have to suffice. The mice had been at it again, but we were unable to find any holes in the rooms, where they were getting in. The first thing I had to do was put the mice poison down. Yvonne had given me some on our previous visit and if this failed to work I decided that I would get one of the men to set a trap. Next, I checked the loft where I had stored several cardboard boxes of bed linen and two duvets. When I opened the first cardboard box, the new duvet was smothered in bits of black plastic bags. On further examination, a large nest shaped hole could be seen, lined with bits of black plastic bag. The duvet, complete with the mouse nest had to be thrown away, together with new fitted bed sheet and tablecloth. After cleaning up the devastation caused by the mice, I went to make up the beds and there I found a sight to behold. The landing was smothered in bees although fortunately they were all dead. This left me wondering where the swarm had gained access into the house which after closer examination seemed to point to a gap above the window frame on the landing which David had forgotten to seal. Joan and I set about cleaning everything in sight before preparing our meal for the evening. That night we had roast lamb and apple pie for pud, which went down well after sandwiches on the journey. Eventually we got around to making up the beds when Joan yelled "come Jill look at the size of this spider - thank goodness it is in your bed and not mine" I ran over to the bedroom and for once she was not exaggerating - it was big. I didn't like these chaps either but I could not show my fear in front of Joan so I quickly got the mop and hit him but he got away although after a search we found him cowering in the corner. This time I swotted him with a book to finish him off after which I got some loo paper and flushed him down the toilet. That night I must admit I lay awake thinking about the various creepy crawlers we had seen and hoped they had all departed. The next day Joan and I went collecting flowers to place in the empty inglenook fireplace to impress any potential buyers. I had already treated myself to a pretty blue and yellow vase to tone with the wall colouring in the lounge. There is always an abundance of wild flowers near the house - unlike England were most of the wild flowers have all but disappeared. Joan suggested we go and buy a piece of matting to go in front of the back door she thought it may prevent some of the mud getting into the house, as the door mat was not man enough for the job. Joan measured from the back door to the beginning of the stairs and went into town to look for a suitable piece. We soon found a piece of mat of the right colour and returned home with our purchase very pleased with ourselves. However, Joan's precise measurements consisted of a mixture of inches and centimetres and included a blank piece on the tape measure about which she was told, resulting in a shortfall of about one foot.

However, I must say this piece of matting served its purpose and saved us a lot of cleaning. Whilst in town we bought some cakes from the patisserie to have with our cup of tea when we got back. I made the tea and we called the men in from next door and we all sat down to enjoy our tea and pastries. Les said casually "Jill look at the mouse on that new rug over there " "Don't be silly - oh! - So there is " I said. He was not joking since there, as bold as brass, was a little shrew cleaning its whiskers. " Oh don't kill him" I said. On closer scrutiny he looked dopey having probably taken some of the mice bait. David scooped him up on a shovel and went outside with him. This sighting left me wondering if it was this little varmint who had made the hole in my settee cover.

That evening we heard a knock at the front door, which proved to be our first visitors to look over the house. The family consisted of the man and wife and their two sons. They told us that they came from England and had seen the property on the Internet and were anxious to look over it. The lady was small but heavy and obviously the boss of the family as husband had a job to get in a word. I offered them a cup of tea and during the conversation we learnt that the husband was on the League of Hospital Friends committee at a hospital for which I had been responsible. Yet again we realised what a small world it was. This reminded my husband and I of the occasion when some years previously, we were travelling in the French Alps in the late evening eventually, finding a remote hotel where we could stay. During the course of the evening meal a man and women at the next table overheard our conversation with the waitress. We had been trying to ask the name of a small animal that we believed to be a marmot but she had insisted that it must have been a lapin (rabbit). The man at the next table interrupted by saying that there were marmots in the mountains. We talked at some length with this gentleman and his wife. We learned from him that, during the Second World War he was with the Free French in my home village in England and he remembered General De Gaulle's vehicle knocking down the sunblind of my Grandmother's shop. I wonder what she would have said about this chance meeting 60 years afterwards with the driver of the vehicle.

Returning to the present, we showed our visitors round the house. However, I could tell from their lack of interest that they were not really firm buyers for our house since they had already seen eight properties before viewing ours - so what difference would one more make - needless to say we did not hear any more from them.

The following day the weather was sunny so Joan and I decided to go for a country walk. It is such a luxury to go out of your front door without immediately having to be aware of speeding road vehicles and to find yourself within seconds surrounded by rolling fields and woodland. We passed a very small church on our walk and found the door unlocked so we went inside to have a look, it was very dark except for the light from two very old stained glass windows, through which the sun poured. It was well cared for and there were fresh flowers on the small altar, you could detect the smell of bee's wax from the well-worn pews. On leaving the church we passed some fishermen by the side of the lake who wished us bon jour as we passed by. We remarked on the appearance of contentment as they waited silently for the fish to bite, with the stillness of the lake reflecting the blue sky - completing the scene of peaceful tranquillity. This reminded me of a poem learnt at school which read 'a poor life this, if full of care, we have no time to stand and stare'.

Arriving home, Joan prepared lunch and I made ready the table outside because the weather was so warm and sunny, we thought it would be a tragedy to eat inside. We had just eaten our lunch when two more visitors arrived and my first impression was that I liked them. They lived in the UK on the south coast near Poole and had property in France in the Loire valley. They had bought it with another couple and the arrangement was not working out, so they were looking for somewhere to buy on their own. They were very taken with the way we had renovated the house and asked to look over it again. They seemed genuinely interested and asked many questions but explained they needed to sell the other property to enable them to buy our house. We found out that they had not booked in anywhere for the night so we took them to the Relais hotel at Josselin where we had stayed when we were looking for property. We arrived at the hotel where they were able to have a room for the night and we bid our farewells, hoping to see them again.

The following day Joan and I went to do some shopping in Ploermel. Joan wanted to buy some post cards to send home and whilst she was doing this, I spotted a print of the sea with sailing boats and two traditional, windswept, whitewashed Breton cottages in the background. This I thought would look just right on the wall in the salon so I bought it. We went into the boulangerie to buy a couple of baguettes and on the way home Joan said "lets do as the French do and break off the end of the baguettes to eat now" "not me" I declared " I dislike indigestion". Joan proceeded to take the end off the baguette and pop it into her mouth but within seconds she exclaimed " Oh look what has happened - my crown has come off". To make things worse, it was one of her front teeth. Joan was embarrassed because it spoilt her smile. Les suggested that we go and ask Mimi the name of a suitable dentist. When we reached Mimi's bar, it was closed. Joan suggested that we go to the pharmacy, as the pharmacist would probably know were the nearest dentist was. I went into the pharmacy, whilst Joan and Les remained in the car. She did not want to speak to the pharmacist without her tooth. I asked him if there was a dentist in Taupont and he said "non - dans Ploermel" I asked him if he could tell me the name of the road where the dental surgery was. He asked me to wait one moment. He went away and came back carrying a page torn from the local telephone directory, with several dentist names. I thanked him for his help and he asked in perfect English if I knew how to get there. When I said that I would ask someone, he said "I have a better idea I will ring my dentist and make an appointment for you" He made an appointment for the next afternoon and gave me directions of where to find it. I thanked him for his kindness and went back out to the car.

When we arrived back home we had only been in for a few minutes and a large 4x4 vehicle pulled up and someone knocked on the door. I opened the door to be met by a sea of faces consisting of two adult couples and numerous children, all wishing to look round the house. I invited them to come in and told them to look around whilst I called my husband to help answer any questions. Les like me was a little surprised at the number of people but they were all polite and wiped their feet - thank goodness. It was like an army tramping over my newly polished floor. They asked many questions about the property but did say they were looking at several others.

On the Wednesday Les and I went into Malestroit to see the agents who were selling the house. We were concerned that there had not been an offer for the house, despite many people coming to see it whilst we were there. We had decided to reduce the price on advice from the agent. We discussed the lack of progress and said we were unhappy with the one person's attitude because on more than one occasion he had been to busy to show potential customers round, making it necessary for us to contact the next door neighbour to show them round. This was difficult because our neighbour did not speak any English and if the potential buyers were unable to speak in French, we could miss a sale. Also the agent had delivered the key to our neighbour and had failed to collect it back. This was some three weeks ago thus making it impossible for the agent to escort potential buyers since the neighbour had been away. When we reached the agents office we were told that the boss was not there because he had been delayed with a Notaire. We were referred to his assistant who was English but in whom we had less confidence and we did not like his manner. Les talked with him at length and said he was not happy with the progress being made on the sale of the house and asked why had they not yet collected their key back from our neighbour. He made some excuse that it had only been there a few days which was not the truth. We asked him to reduce the asking price on his brochures, which he agreed to do. When we left his office, we found a key cutting shop and had two more sets of keys made and then delivered one set back to the agent.

I had to get back quickly because I was taking Joan to the dentist. We arrived at the dental surgery on time I rang the doorbell and the door was opened promptly by a small very pleasant lady with brown piercing eyes. I explained who we were and that Joan had lost her crown. I suggested to Joan that she should show where her crown had been, which she did in response to which the lady quickly laughed and exclaimed ` Dracula' and we could not help seeing the funny side of it. We were shown into a sparsely furnished room which I presumed was the waiting room, although there were no other patients waiting and Joan was soon called into the surgery. I browsed through the books on the table, but could not find anything to interest me as they were either children's books or magazines on fishing. I had been waiting for Joan about half an hour when the doorbell went again and another patient arrived. The little French lady explained to the man that the dentist had an emergency and he would be kept waiting for a short time. The man came in and sat down took one look at the books and also decided they were not for him. He sat back in his chair and proceeded to nod off. Some time later the little lady reappeared and beckoned to me saying" would you come and interpret". Although I quickly explained my French was not that good, I was led into the surgery. This room was large but appeared very cluttered. The dentist had his back to me and did not utter one word, when I said" Bon Jour". Joan, who was sitting in the dental chair looking very flushed and agitated. She was very worried about the treatment. She said "Jill can you explain to the dentist that I don't want him to file my denture down". I replied saying "how do you think I can tell him that". I could not think what French was for denture or file and who was I to tell the dentist what to do anyway. My brain was desperately trying to think what to say. This situation was proving more difficult by the minute since Joan would not understand French anyway, I decided to try and change the subject. I was more concerned to find out the cost of the treatment. I said to the French lady, who by now I realised was the receptionist/nurse "do we need to complete the form E111" which enables British subjects to reclaim medical costs for treatment in France. On later reflection, I realised that this treatment in the UK would probably not be covered on the NHS anyway. The receptionist looked at me blankly so I produced the form and explained as best I could the part she had to complete and the part Joan would have to sign. I had great difficulty in making her understand that the document must have the stamp on it with the dentist's name. When I had gone through the motions of stamping the document she realised at last what I meant and we were all smiles again. I asked her what the cost for the new crown would be. She muttered something to the dentist and then quoted a figure of 450 francs (which was £45). I thought this was very reasonable and explained to Joan what the cost of the crown would be. She replied " I hope I can pay by card since I haven't got that much in cash". I asked madame if we could pay by card. Before she could utter a word a voice behind me said" Non Carte - cash". Joan nearly fell off the chair. My face must have shown my amazement at the sound of his voice and I was thinking to myself he had understood all along what we had been saying to each other. Between us we came up with the money and as quick as we could we made our exit. Joan said the treatment was good but he had no idea of aseptic technique. When he had been filing her denture down he kept blowing on it to remove the dust then wiping it on his coat. However she still had the crown in-situ two years on.

On the Friday Les bought some paint for me to paint the doors and windows outside of the house he said it would keep me out of mischief and make the house outside look as good as inside. We returned home the following Tuesday and I must say the house looked really desirable and I was very sad to be selling it. I realised we could not keep all three houses but Pré du lac was so comfortable. As we were returning to the UK, we realised that the house was looking just as we had visualised it would be, when we had first entered into the venture.

When we returned to France in July, on the second day of our stay a lady came to view the house, explaining that she had already visited the house with the agent but she had come back for a second look around. She asked many questions and appeared very interested. We learnt that she and her husband lived in Ireland where they had a farm. They were looking for somewhere quiet for holidays and thought our house would be ideal, but the problem would be getting a mortgage. We hoped they would be successful because she seemed a very appropriate person and would make a good neighbour. Being a farmer's wife, she would readily fit in to the farming community here. When she departed she said she hoped we would meet up again and would ring us if they could get a mortgage, unfortunately we did not here from her again.

The following day more visitors arrived from Weymouth to see the house. They asked about the cost of living here. They also wanted details of the taxes that had to be paid on French property. My husband explained that we pay two taxes on the house, namely Taxes Foncières and Taxe D'Habitation but the total of these is probably less than UK Council Tax. They asked if we would accept payment for the sale of the house in Francs and we said that we would. They deflated our hopes for a sale however, when they said that they would try to get a mortgage. They spent some time looking round the garden with me and I apologised for the height of the grass but explained that we would be buying a strimmer and that was our next job to cut the grass down. I did mention to them to be careful in the long grass because there was the occasional snake. Oh! you should have seen Les's face which was a picture when I mentioned snakes. If looks could kill, I would have been 6ft under. He quickly said " We have not seen any yet and we have been here two and a half years but they do have them further down the south of France". I said, digging myself deeper into the mire, "there is one nasty snake - the viper, but all the pharmacies round here carry the anti venom injection". When they departed Les said "do you want to sell the house or not - SNAKES ALIVE- how stupid can you be telling people that there are snakes in the garden" We all started to giggle I must admit it was stupid but it just came out.

The evening before we were due to leave, the others had gone to bed. I was sitting alone in the salon, thinking how sad it was to sell this house. My thoughts wandered back to when the walls and ceilings, were festooned with cobwebs. The neglected polished wooden beech floor was damp and had some woodworm. The fireplace was in need of repair and the damp walls were in need of re-plastering. The surfaces of the two hundred years old beams were pitted with woodworm holes.

Looking at the room that night, I could hardly believe how much we had changed its appearance. The floor now shone like a ballroom, the walls were plastered and painted in a pale primrose colour, the fireplace was restored and its original stone chimney was repointed. The beams had been returned to their former glory by sandblasting and wood treatment. The downstairs bathroom previously colourless and drab, now was bright and cheerful, with apricot walls and curtains to match. The tiles shone after being thoroughly cleaned, toning in with the painted walls.

There was now a kitchen where the animals had been kept. The dirt floor was now concreted and tiled and the bare stonewalls which had been full of spiders cobwebs and other incumbents, were now plastered. There were new ceiling boards laid on the original beams. A hard wood window in keeping with the outward appearance of the building had replaced the old ventilation slot in the wall. There were bright curtains hanging at the window through which the early morning sun streamed, lighting up the whole room. The white kitchen cupboards and appliances gave the feeling of space.

The wide front and back doors had been replaced with doors we had made from solid mahogany. We kept the original bar type hinges, which had been given a new lease of life by cleaning and the application of a coat of black paint. There was now a staircase up to the first floor, replacing the original homemade loft ladder that had collapsed under my husband's weight. We had made a balustrade to fit around the top of the stairs and create a spacious landing. At one end of this a floor to ceiling window had replaced a large old granary door. This had been enhanced by my turquoise and rose curtains. The landing floor was now new polished wood and in one corner I had placed the little old bench, cleaned and polished, which I had found in the fireplace downstairs. Under this window Les had made a plinth and upon this I sat a large vase of regularly replaced flowers.

Leading from the landing were four bedrooms and a shower room. New windows had been made in the bedrooms to give more light. The light was previously from very small holes in the stonework, through which birds flew in and out at their leisure. These small holes now had glass panes in them.

The wooden floors in two of the bedrooms were new. I had stained these and had now placed brightly coloured mats upon them. All the upstairs walls were white, with the furnishings supplying the colour and brightness to the rooms. The other two bedrooms still had the original floor for which we had hired a sander to remove the roughened top surfaces. This had not been easy to stain since they were not tongued and groved, although they now looked acceptable. The shower and toilet room was blue and white.

With the benefit of hindsight, we wished that we had utilised the second floor loft space. The high-pitched roof provided adequate headroom for two further bedrooms had we put in a wood floor above the bedrooms instead of plasterboard ceilings.

We decided to store this thought for our next project.

When we had settled back in England, we were still receiving calls about our French property from people who had seen it on the Internet. Between the time we had arrived home and our next tip in October we had received 24 calls from potential buyers. Several people had asked if we would rent the property. When the property had been on the market for five months, we decided to let it out to some friends for a holiday which would bring in a small income which was well below the price for this time of the year as they were friends. The only other people to rent the house, were friends of Les and he was the chief project manager on a new building project in the UK. Laughingly he had said that if they had any potential buyers whilst they were there, they would flog it for us - no problem. During their stay, they were outside cooking a barbecue when two people arrived to view the house. Trevor showed them round and did his very best to promote the property and he must have done a good sales pitch because they came back twice again during his holiday and decided to buy it. He claimed that his expertise with the barbecue had been a contributory factor.

We subsequently exchanged contracts with these viewers and completed the sale by the middle of November 2000.

CHAPTER SEVENTEEN

Was it worth it?

We were sitting quietly by the fireside when the telephone call confirmed that the sale of Pré du Lac had been completed. Obviously we had mixed feelings after receiving this news. On the one hand we were relieved to know that we would now have sufficient money to carry out the renovation of the other two houses. On the other hand we were both sad to be leaving the house where we had achieved so much with the house now so comfortable and pleasant to live in compared with its state when we started. I suppose it was inevitable that we began to wonder whether or not it had been worth the efforts.

On the positive side the renovation of the house in France had been a challenge, giving us a purpose after retiring from busy and responsible jobs. This project had been our answer to the routine and dullness of some people's retirement states. We have been fortunate in the willingness and ability of the many people we chose to employ to help us to carry out the renovations. We all seemed to strike up a wonderful comradeship between each other. There was laughter in the face of difficulties although sometimes preceded by stress or suspense when jobs were in danger of not turning out precisely as we had wished. We had the discipline of working to a self-imposed tight time scale. We were forced into a steep learning curve by the necessity of conducting our transactions almost entirely in French, which gave rise to many amusing incidents. The French people we have come into contact with over this period have convinced us that the French attitudes to life and work is something that we would like to share. The kindness and generosity of our village neighbours towards us has been quite genuine with the hospitality they so readily gave to us and give to each other.

We feel perhaps that we have experienced rural life as it was in England fifty years ago, with wild life at our doorstep and on some occasions over the doorstep. We have appreciated the tranquillity and beauty of the surrounding countryside, with bright sunny mornings and warm balmy evenings. The roads are quiet with no car parking problems or traffic jams. We have, on our days off from work, travelled to nearby towns and villages sight-seeing. We have visited beaches, explored sunny coves and walked along the quiet unspoilt stretches of sand in search of the odd rock pool, hoping to catch a glimpse of one of the inhabitants. We have visited many Chateaux and Churches and looked in wonder at the architecture, learning much about the history of these places and their past occupants.

I have found it very amusing how the local village people never bother to lock their doors when they pop out. This brought childhood memories back to me from the times when I used to stay with my grandparents for summer holidays. My grandmother used to hang the key on the back of the door tied to a piece of string.
When she went out after closing the door she would draw the key on its piece of string through the letterbox and lock the door. After which she would then push the key on its piece of string through the letterbox. She could then unlock the door when we got back. In the meantime an intruder who wanted to open the door and get in the house could do so but no one to my knowledge ever did. How times have changed.

We love the French food and have discovered many mouth watering delicacies, enjoying the odd meal out and I love the leisurely pace of the meals no one rushes you here - you can take your time.

If we ask ourselves was it worth it financially, we can be more precise in our appraisals. The project, namely the purchase, renovation and sale of Pré du Lac, produced the following results
(Figures are in Francs)

Purchase of the house and land	220,000
Labour costs	60,000
Material costs	70,000
Contractors	10,000
Total Cost	360,000
Proceeds after capital gains tax	390,000
Profit	30,000

The above figures do not take into account some related costs such as ferry costs for vehicle and passengers, food during our alternate monthly visits, heating, fuel and entertainment.

House purchasing prices in France although increasing more rapidly, are still substantially lower than those in the UK but the impact of this also applies when selling property in France.

We are now doing it all again hoping that we have learned from some of our previous experiences.

After Renovation